Drug Abuse
Among
Working Children

Drug Abuse Among Working Children

Dr Vimala Veeraraghavan
(Professor, Dept of Applied Psychology)
University of Delhi, South Campus, Delhi

&

Dr Itishree Misra

NORTHERN BOOK CENTRE
Publishers of Scholarly Books
NEW DELHI

ISBN 81-7211-090-1

The project was sponsored by Ministry of Welfare, Govt. of India, New Delhi

Published by Northern Book Centre, 1 Daryaganj, New Delhi 110 002
Ph. 3271626, 3280295; E-mail : nbcnd@ndb.vsnl.net.in; Fax : 011-3252651
and printed at Paragon Enterprises, 4221/1 Ansari Road, New Delhi 110 002,
Phone 3264519

Foreword

The phenomenon of drug abuse is a serious concern not only to the health sector but all sections of our society. Over the last two or three decades, awareness of illicit drugs, access to them and their abuse have dramatically increased. Although reliable and systematic quantification of the problem is not available, there is a general agreement that populations at highest risk are those in the age range of 20-35 which is most needed for creative and productive work.

Pattern of abuse in different countries show enormous variation including drugs abused, individuals who take drugs, various settings and range of impacts. Economically drug abuse consumes tremendous sums of money that cannot be invested in channels of creative and social education and health promotion activities. Often, such easy generation of money leads to various undesirable social, economic and violent crimes.

In drugs, as in economics, demand generates supply. The question is which of the two deserve most of our concern. The answer to this question would be the reduction of the demand side, especially when the future of children is involved.

The present book is the result of the painstaking research undertaken by Professor Vimala Veeraraghavan and her research team who studied this problem in working children. The introduction chapter brings to the fore some of the important measures taken at national and international levels and focuses on the efforts of the Govt. of India regarding this problem which resulted in multi-centred study with a uniform methodology. The book brings to light many issues hitherto ignored, as for instance the easy accessibility of the dangerous drugs like smack to children of less than 10 years of age. It highlights the callous ways in which the contractors exploit young children to work in very exhausting and health harming type of work, and the least concern that they show towards the children's health, education or welfare. The experiences of working children taking drugs and the reasons for their resorting to drugs demonstrate the miserable plight of these young children, and the conditions which drive them out of their homes and force them not only to work but to resort to drugs and alcohol due to exhaustion and lack of any positive alternatives after their work hours. This book is different from other such works mainly in that it has explored the hitherto unexplored area of drug use among working children highlighting the need to immediately do something to overcome the problem. It is unique in suggesting many remedial and rehabilitative measures that are practical and that which could be effectively implemented. The "do's and don'ts for the parents and the various suggested measures including counselling that could be taken up with these children and parents are indeed praiseworthy. Such report should not be left unattended by administrators and planners concerned with drug problem in working children. Rather the report should help in developing implementable plan of action.

In the context of drug problem, another significant issue which I would like to mention is about the increasing consumption of alcohol by youth in the recent past. The use of alcohol and other drugs not only cause harm to an individual but also destroys the whole fabric of the society. The book clearly brings out the fact that the educational emotional social and economic problems due to drug abuse are pervasive, and the existing measures to prevent and control drug abuse are weak and the knowledge base on which these measures rest is even weaker. The recent trends only suggest further deterioration, as timely remedial actions are not taken.

Professor (Dr) Shridhar Sharma
Emeritus Professor & President of
The World Association for Social Psychiatry
Preet Vihar, Delhi

Acknowledgements

The present study has been possible to undertake because of the grant provided by the Ministry of Welfare, Government of India. At the same time, it must be mentioned that but for the cooperation of the working children who have been respondents in this research, it would have been impossible to conduct this type of study. I acknowledge gratefully their cooperation and help. I am particularly indebted to the two children who introduced the research investigators to other working children who were using drugs. My special thanks to all of them.

A work of this type is not possible unless one has a dedicated and committed team of workers. I have been fortunate to have had an excellent research team which worked at all odd hours — sometimes in the early hours and sometimes late at nights — going around all odd places in Delhi with smiling faces. My special appreciation goes to Dr Itishree Mohapatra, Research Officer in this project (co-author of this book) who led the team ably and efficiently and completed the most difficult part of the research, namely data collection on time. In this context I also acknowledge the contribution of Mr Raman Singh who accompanied the research investigators to most areas of Delhi, devoting his valuable time and energy. He encouraged and motivated all the other workers to participate and interact with the working children and spend their time to give them some moments of happiness.

I am grateful to Prof Dr Shridhar Sharma for writing the foreword to this book.

Data entry and typing of the report was very efficiently done by Ms Manjul for which I thank her. Last but not the least my special thanks to Mr Manash Kumar Roy who looked after the accounts and other administrative work of the project and to Mr Braj Kumar for looking after the entire filing and other clerical work.

Prof (Dr) Vimala Veeraraghavan

List of Tables

Contents

Contents

I

Drug Abuse
An Introduction

Drug abuse as a problem has existed for centuries. Its negative effects on human functioning and.abilities have been posing serious concern for the last few decades, as a large number of youngsters and adults in the reproductive age group are getting increasingly involved in this potentially dangerous habit.

In the West, as for instance in the USA, the problem of drug abuse and addiction has become so intense, that to control the use of hardcore addictive drugs, other types of drugs such as marihuana have to be used. Many stringent legal measures have been introduced to handle this almost uncontrollable problem. Treatment centres and deaddiction centres have been opened in many cities, and rehabilitation centres have been started for drug addicts who are jobless and abandoned by their families.

At the international level, many high level meetings and workshops have been held under the aegis of UNESCAP, USAID, ONCB and other global organizations to find ways and means to overcome this problem which has also started spreading its wings all over Asia, the more affected countries being India, Thailand, Pakisthan, and Ceylon.

The control of drug abuse requires, among other things, factual data on personal characteristics of drug users, information on drugs that are more commonly used, and the methods used in the ingestion of drugs. Also, information on the nature and effects of drugs and the knowledge of these two factors among the users, the age group involved in taking drugs, and the reasons thereof, the place where the drug takers choose to meet, the sources from which the drugs are obtained, persons who acts as drug pushers, etc. is needed. Another area in which information is required is the attitude of the drug takers towards deaddiction and rehabilitation measures that are available in the country and their motivation to get rid of the life-damaging and life-killing drug habit.

As noted by the ESCAP (1990) workshop on "Drug Abuse in the ESCAP region" : (i) useful data on drug abuse is very difficult to obtain for many reasons of which one is that drug abuse being illegal, it is difficult to identify a drug abuser; (ii) the drug abuse pattern changes so frequently that it is difficult to monitor the same; and (iii) the demarcating line between abuse of licit and illicit drugs is not clear and hence difficult to define. Furthermore, certain drugs have legitimate medical use and thus to detect addiction to these drugs the level of intake has to reach a very high frequency and intensity. In addition to all the above , there is also an inherent conflict between the development of a data a system for enforcement purposes and the development of a system to serve prevention programmes. The workshop noted that the drugs were not abused where they were not available or accessible. Hence the control efforts have to be in those areas where drugs are available or easily accessible.

Causes

Causes for drug abuse behaviour are many, complex and unrelated. It is not a medical problem but the one in which medical considerations are secondary to economic ones. Among the causes for drug intake, social, economic and psychological factors play an important role. The social factors include changes in the value and belief systems in the society, splitting of families because of migration, changes in techniques of production and exposure to alternative life-style through media and communication technology, as well as high competition in the field of education. Contemporary social and economic changes have been a few of the underlying factors in the dynamic process of a society, adversely affecting the rich as well as the poor, by weakening the family system and relationship. In other words, inflexible child rearing practices which do not take into consideration, the changing social, psychological and cultural milieu, may tend to render children vulnerable to the appeal of all kinds of deviant behaviours including drug abuse.

It has been recognised since long that drug abuse needs a multi-approach system for handling and this aspect needs to be kept in mind while chalking out developmental plans to deal with social problems of this nature. Although it has been widely accepted that prevention of initiation of drug abuse and providing treatment and rehabilitation facilities for drug abusers is potentially the most effective method to deal with the problem, it is heartening to note that many voluntary organizations are implementing the same quite adequately. According to the survey done by ESCAP (1990), 40% of the various projects taken by different organizations were in the area of information dissemination. Next in order were the projects that focused on training, alternative activities, education and research. There were a very small number of projects which were concerned with legislation, publication of narcotics periodicals and counselling. The target was the general public, in-school and out-of-school youths, parents and tribals. Although these prevention programmes are stated to be effective, experience shows that success with children who are already drug addicts is negligible because of their tender age and lack of understanding of repercussion of this habit. Even if they appear to be aware of the consequences of drug intake, they continue to indulge in the habit for various reasons like : a way to overcome certain conflicts, opportunity to behave like an adult, to overcome the compounded fear, to soothen the pain of rapid change, to avoid physical pain, to compensate for the parental inadequacies such as marital problems between the parents which force the parents at times to remain insensitive and unintentionally neglectful towards the child. In some children it is a reinforced behaviour to get exorbitant power by taking drugs, parents being the introducers. Thus drug abuse has become almost an insurmountable problem and it has become essential to intervene at different levels to overcome the same, keeping the external factors such as rapid change in every walk of life, availability of drugs etc., constant.

The specific solution to drug dependency cannot be divorced from the general problem of personality development. The more we learn how to meet our children's legitimate needs the less they will resort to illegal modes of gratification. The more self-dependent, the less drug dependence and the more self direction, the less the chemical escape. Therefore the best guard against drug abuse are attitudes and skills that allow us to remain human and helpful even when we make demands, set limits, and insist that youngsters follow the prescribed values. As a parent, one is expected to help children develop certain essential skills in them which would not only help them to overcome their difficulties, but also prevent them from getting into deviant behaviours including drug abuse. However, it is seen that both at higher and lower socio-economic strata as well as in the case of working and non working parents, unintended neglect and economic insecurity and the need for subsistent level earnings, make parents drive away their children from home as is obtained in a large number of cases of working children. Many parents want their children to work and earn while others not being in a position to look after them, make them go away from home or neglect them to such an extent that the children get into bad company or fall into traps of exploiting contractors who employ them for a minimal wage and keep them under their control. The problem of drug abuse among working children is thus a phenomenon which needs to be studied in depth and understood. A few of the important issues related to drug abuse among working children are presented in the following section.

Drug Abuse Among Working Children

Economic exploitation of children in India has always existed and appears to have increased over the years. The Census of India 1981 estimated that there were 13.17 million child workers below the age of fourteen, engaged mostly in rural agricultural activities. The National Sample Survey in 1983 estimated that there were 17.36 million child workers in the age group of 5 to 15 years. The Operations Research Group placed the figure at 14 million in 1985. Most of these children work under stressful conditions in agriculture, and other industries, often hazardous. Some are "bonded" labourers and a few girl children are even sold into prostitution. The Planning Commission estimates that there would be around 20 million working children by the year AD 2000.

India has several million children living under especially difficult circumstances. These include for instance, an estimated 500,000 street children in seven cities: Bangalore, Mumbai, Calcutta, Delhi, Hyderabad, Kanpur and Chennai. Majority of these children are over eight years of age, have never attended school, and have parents who are on low paid unskilled jobs. Similarly there is very little information available about children of fisherfolk, the disabled children, and children affected by riots and disasters, all of whom fall under the category of "children in especially difficult circumstance" (UNICEF, 1994)

According to the statistics on children in India (NIPCCD, 1994) 111.69 million children between 0-14 years are main workers, that is, one who has worked for the major part of the year preceding the date of enumeration; in other words, those children who were engaged in any economically productive activity for 183 days or 6 months or more during the year. There are 24.24 million children who are marginal workers in the same age group. Of the total children as main workers, those working as cultivators were 4.013 million (35.92%) as agricultural labourers were 4.774 million (42.74%), as workers in allied activities such as fisheries etc. 7.04 lakh (6.3%), 27000 worked in mining and quarrying occupations (0.24%), 4.25 lakh worked in the manufacturing industry (3.8%), 5.41 lakh were working in industries other than household ones (4.84%), 80,000 were working as construction workers (0.71%), and children working in trade and commerce occupations were 2.45 lakh (2.19%). These figures do not include working children in marginal occupations.

Among child population those who were convicted for criminal type activities were in all 21.358 million, which is nearly twice the number involved in different types of occupations. Within the varied types of criminal activities, there were only 23,000 who were apprehended for dealing with narcotic drugs, 1.863 million were apprehended under the Prohibition Act, namely for dealing in alcoholic drinks etc. This number may also include children who are in varied types of occupations.

The problem of drug abuse is not unique in the sense that it has been a feature of all societies in the world since time immemorial and is considered to have arisen out of therapeutic and hedonisitc considerations and in some cases as a means of escape from the reality of life's stresses and strains. The substances used for intoxication/addictive purposes have also varied from society to society and from time to time depending upon the development of science and technology. Of the various substances, the ones that have survived from ancient times to today are alcohol, cannabis and opium and these still form the hard core of the drug problem.

Before dealing with different kinds of drugs, it will be in order to define "Drug" which has been variously defined by experts, scholars and organizations. The WHO defined drug as a "substance that, when taken in the living organism, may modify one or more of its functions." Drug abuse has three stages: (1) the individual takes a drug for certain specific immediate results which he values, often inspite of a clear awareness of its adverse effects in the long run; (2) the individual tends to repeat the drug to re-experience the pleasurable sensations while others continue to experience similar effects at the same dose or frequency; (3) as the drug use is continued over a period of time it leads to complex biochemical relationship in the body of the individual and in the absence of intake of the drug the individual develops certain distresssing psychological and physical symptoms called as "withdrawal symptoms" that are usually drug specific.

Studies on Drug Abuse in India

There have been numerous studies on drug abuse in India and in the more recent times the Ministry of Welfare has sponsored multicentred studies with a common methodology so as to obtain the needed information on this problem at an all India level. Though still inadequate to ascertain the magnitude of the drug problem, these efforts have resulted in obtaining to an extent the prevalence rate of drug abuse in India. Many studies have also been undertaken by individual experts, academicians and practitioners to understand the specific aspects related to drug abuse.

Analysis of patterns of drug use and abuse has shown that there had been a radical and steady increase in the drug abuse until the year 1981 and then a drop in the same substituted by more serious drugs such as heroin, barbiturates etc. (Mohan, Sethi and Tongue, 1981). In India, though it has been acknowledged that there has been a fall in the drug abuse phenomenon in the 1980s compared to the 1970s, there is no authentic statistics to support this contention. As for studies earlier to 1977 on drug abuse, the report on drug addiction in India by the Ministry of Health presents a fairly thorough review and as for studies after that period, one may refer to the multicentred study published by the Ministry of Welfare in 1992. The important findings of this study were:

- Drug addiction is prevalent in varying degrees among all religious and caste groups. Most drug abusers were literate and the age group most affected was between 16-35 years.
- A significant proportion of addicts came from the lower strata and a large number of them were labourers, transport workers and student youth.
- The most commonly abused drugs were cannabis and heroin.
- Peer pressure and curiosity were found to be the main factors in drug abuse.
- The common source of supply of drugs comprised drug peddlars and pushers who operated through petty shopkeepers and pan-wallahs.
- There was widespread awareness of the ill effects of the drugs in both individuals and their family members.

- In industrial areas, the availability of drugs is rather conspicuous, and with the inflow of migrants from rural areas and other states in search of gainful employment the drug abuse problem has become more complex.
- Because of ignorance and inadaptability, the young people from the villages etc. fall an easy prey to the nefarious elements indulging in drug trafficking.
- It was found that though drug addiction has its origin in sheer curiosity, the continuance of this habit is a conscious decision on the part of the drug abuser.

The inferences one may draw from the many studies mentioned above are :

- The existing studies in India do not cover all the states and the ones available on the general population or on a specific target group such as students or industrial workers are mainly cross sectional in nature and not representatives of the population.
- Many of the findings based on the research conducted by different individuals and experts are not comparable because of the different methodologies adopted by them.
- Most studies have invariably focused on the socio-demographic features of the drug abuse population and the drugs used for the purpose.
- By and large almost all the studies have arrived at the conclusion that the most frequently used drugs are tobacco, alcohol, cannabis, and smack to an extent. Psychotropic drugs were found to be used rarely, perhaps because of their non-availability or inaccessibility.
- The proportion of users to nonusers was very small though a slight increase in this proportion has been observed in some studies.

At the opening plenary meeting (ESCAP, 1990) which reviewed the drug abuse situation in Asia and the Pacific region, the meeting of senior officials had before it three documents concerning the drug abuse situation and these were:

(i) The drug abuse demand situation in Asia and the Pacific region;
(ii) Report on trends in the illicit traffic of narcotic drugs and psychotropic substances in the region of Asia and the Pacific;
(iii) Illicit drug trafficking and money laundering.

In the report submitted to the ESCAP meeting, the drug situation as prevailing in Mumbai was described. It was pointed out that in 1980-81, a crude form of heroin (brown sugar) was introduced into the city and that 81% of the users of brown sugar were in the age group of 11-26 years.

As regards drug abuse among industrial workers, nothing significant was obtained. Studies by Mohan and others indicated that drug abuse appeared to be present even among very young school-going children. According to the study by Veeraraghavan (1992), the main age group affected was 15-30 years and the main drug used was smack, and in some cases cannabis, opium, cocaine etc. The main sources of supply of drugs were found to be the Sansi tribe, peddlars, pushers in various resettlement and crowded colonies of Delhi; *pan* and cigarrette shops, *dhabas* in certain areas; and resettlement and "juggi-jhompri" colonies.

The occupational group most affected included the transport workers, bus and truck drivers and conductors, TSR drivers, rickshaw pullers; pickpockets and ragpickers. Thus most drug related problems seem to be in these occupational groups. In the study by Mohan, et al., (1981) it was found that out of a sample of 1,192 boys and 840 girls from classes IX, X and XI, painkiller was used by a large percentage of students (49%), followed by alcohol (12.7%), tobacco (6%), tranquilizers (3.5%) and less than 0.5% used the rest of the drugs. The largest number of student users of drugs were from class IX, followed by students of classes X & XI respectively.

Thus the problem of drug abuse has been found to be present among the youngsters who are in schools or colleges and from 'well-off' families. However, there has been no study as yet focused on child workers.

Before looking into the drug use or abuse behaviour among child workers, it is important to consider some of the facts related to child labour in India as well as understand the occupations in which children are working and the possibilities of drug abuse among them.

Employment of children is nothing new in India and the condition of poverty has forced a large number of parents to use their children for varied types of work so as to supplement the family income. However, under pressure from the Human Rights Commission many NGOs' international organizations such as the ILO has made the Government of India to prohibit child labour in the country. While many laws prohibiting child labour exist in India, implementation has always been a problem. Keeping this in view, the Government of India following up on a preliminary notification issued on 26th may 1993 as part of the child labour Prohibition and Regulation Act, 1986, prohibited employment of children in many occupations in addition to the ones that already existed.

The occupations presently prohibited include, abattoirs, slaughter houses; hazardous processes as defined in S.(2cb) and "dangerous operations" as notified under rules made with reference to S.87 of the Factory Act, 1948 (63 of 1948); "printing" as defined in S.2(k) (iv) of the Factory Act (63 of 1948); cashew and cashew nut descaling and processing and "soldering" - processes in electronics industries.

Thus the Child Labour Act, 1986 prohibits children from being employed, in any work except in the family based work or recognised school based activities. Further, children if at all they work, can be permitted to work only for 6 hours in the permitted occupations and that too neither before 8 A.M. nor after 7 P.M.

The Government of India announced the National policy on child labour in August, 1987. The action plan under the National Child labour policy comprises (i) a legislative action plan; (ii) focusing of general development programmes for benefiting children where ever possible; and (iii) project-based action plans in areas of high concentration of child labour engaged in wage/quasi-wage employment.

In the year 1995-96, the Planning Commission allotted Rs 34.40 crore for implementation of 12 national labour projects to eliminate child labour in hazardous occupations altogether by AD 2000. During 1994-95, financial assistance was given to 11 voluntary organizations in the field of child labour for implementation of continuing as well as starting of new projects for the welfare of working children so as, to provide them non-formal education, supplementary nutrition, health care and vocational skill training.

As for Delhi, which was the setting for this research, according to 1981 census figures, there were about 26000 working children in Delhi of which 24855 were main workers and 862 in marginal occupations. According to NIPCCD (1992), a working child is an easy victim for drug peddlars. They earn and so have money to spend on drugs. The modus operandi of peddlars is to befriend the children when they seem to be lonely and unhappy. They persuade them to take one puff of the smack telling them that it would make them feel better in order to get them hooked on to the drug. According to this study the age group of these working children was 9 to 12 years in about two-thirds of the cases. In a survey of trends in drug use of Indian adolescents living on reservations, Beauvois, et al. (1985) pointed out that several detrimental conditions prevalent in living areas, unemployment, prejudice and lack of optimism about the future were all responsible for the increase in drug abuse among them.

While child labour as a problem has been studied and handled to quite an extent in India, the hidden problem of drug use and abuse among these working children has not been looked into. Finding that drug use is becoming increasingly alarming among youngsters and particularly the working children, the Government of India, Ministry of Welfare, using a common methodology decided that this problem be studied in detail in different parts of the country one of which was Delhi.

Thus the present research has focused on understanding the phenomenon of drug abuse among working children, with particular emphasis on the types of drugs used by them, the money spent by them on drugs, the intensity and frequency of intake of these drugs, the effects that the drugs have on them and their awareness regarding the dangerous consequences of using drugs, etc.

It is hoped that this study, which is a pioneering effort, would be able to throw light on some of the major factors related to this problem which is affecting a large number of young people. The study also tries to find ways and means to prevent drug use and abuse amongst these children.

The next chapter deals with the methodology used in this study.

II

Certain Methodological Considerations

As mentioned in the previous chapter, the main purpose of this research was to study the phenomenon of drug abuse among working children and to formulate effective strategies of intervention for its eradication.

Thus more specifically, the objectives of the research were as follows:

- To assess the extent of drug use among working children.
- To identify the various drugs used by them.
- To ascertain the frequency of drug consumption among them.
- To investigate as to how the affected children get introduced to drugs.
- To know how long it takes the affected child to get addicted to drugs.
- To know how much money the affected children spend on drugs, and in case their expenditure on drugs exceed their earnings, where do they get the extra money from.
- To identify the effects of drug abuse among the affected children.
- To study how the working children cope with the ill effects of drugs.
- To find the family background of the working children who abuse drugs.

- To study how the families cope with the problems created by drug abuse by their working children.
- To investigate whether there is any identifiable relationship between the use of drugs by working children and the working condition.
- To find whether the children affected by drugs are aware of de-addiction facilities available in their localities or elsewhere.
- To find whether the affected persons are willing to submit themselves to de-addiction procedure and get rehabilitated.
- To suggest, on the basis of the study, possible intervention strategies to prevent drug abuse among working children.

Research Design

For the purpose of this study, an exploratory research design was used as nothing was known about the phenomenon of drug use or abuse among working children. As such no specific hypothesis could be laid down except for certain broad assumptions based on the available literature and personal experience of conducting research in the area of drug abuse.

The assumptions were as follows:

Since working children generally stay away from their homes and parents, they are more vulnerable to exploitation by the drug pushers and sellers who force them to sell drugs. In the process many children fall an easy prey to drug taking habits.

Secondly, after working throughout the day, working children have little opportunity to play or have any kind of recreation. Hence they are more susceptible to becoming an easy prey to many suggestions to take drugs so as to feel relaxed etc.

Thirdly, usually the work is so tiring, that children start taking drug to forget their aches and pains and in the process run the risk of getting addicted.

Fourthly, the easy availability of drugs and lack of any legal or other sanctions and the absence of any parental control leads the children to get hooked on to the drugs.

Sample

For the purpose of this study, Delhi has been divided into 5 zones i.e. East, West, North, South, and Central Delhi. In each of these areas the following places were visited to have a first-hand experience of meeting working children and study their drug-addiction habits.

- Teashops at major bus stands, railway stations, bus terminals, road intersections, etc.
- Canteens run by public and private organizations, in university campuses and colleges, at cinema theaters, factories and industrial settings.
- Dhabas and motels on the roadside, small hotels and restaurants.
- The carpet industry, the electronic, textiles, and other industries and auto repair garages.

The study was conducted in two phases. The first phase was to survey the areas listed above and obtain information on the number of working children. From among them using a specially devised checklist, children who use or abuse drugs were identified.

The second phase involved detailed interviews with the working children identified as drug users/abusers.

Since in the first phase it was found that the children were reluctant to give any information during their working hours or in front of their parents, guardians contractors or any elders, they were interviewed in different parks and temples where they generally spent their evening taking drugs. The

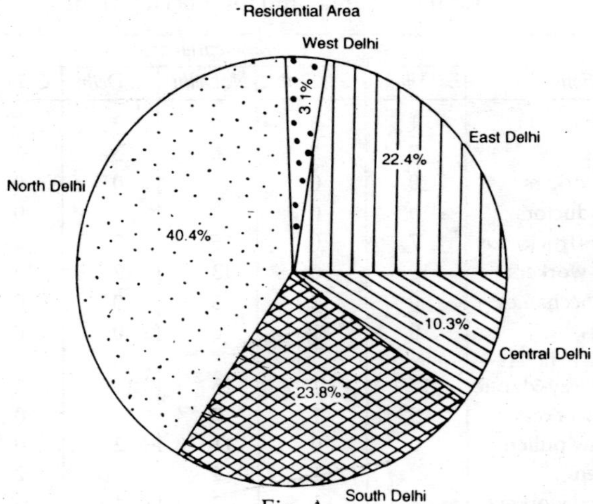

Fig. A

research investigators befriended some of the drug addicted children who in turn directed them to other working children who used drugs. Thus, altogether 223 drug addicted children were identified and interviewed. The largest number of working children were interviewed in North Delhi, followed by South Delhi, East Delhi, Central Delhi and West Delhi in that order (see Fig. A). The number of working children interviewed in different residential areas in terms of their occupations is given in Table A:

According to perception and statement of the children, these occupations have also been categorized according to their degree of difficulty while analysing the results.

Tools used for Data Collection

The research being an exploratory one, the main tool used for data collection was a questionnaire specially devised for the purpose, keeping in mind the various objectives set down for the study. In addition to this, a checklist was prepared so as to identify abusers among the working children.

Table A Distribution of working children in different residential areas and their occupations

	Residential areas					
Occupations	*E. Delhi*	*W. Delhi*	*N. Delhi*	*S. Delhi*	*C. Delhi*	*Total*
Kabadis	1	0	9	3	3	16
Vendors	2	2	6	3	3	16
Agril. workers	0	0	1	0	0	1
Bus conductors	10	0	1	1	0	12
Cleaners truck/bus	7	0	5	10	0	22
Factory workers	10	0	13	2	10	35
Motor mechanics	0	0	3	0	0	3
Servants	0	1	0	0	0	1
Workers in hotel/ motel/ wayside cafe	12	1	25	11	2	51
Skilled workers	5	1	9	8	0	23
Rickshaw pullers	0	0	11	2	0	13
Salesmen	0	1	4	9	2	16
Unskilled workers	3	1	3	4	3	14
Total	50	7	90	53	23	223

The checklist covered the basic demographic factors of the working child and his family, and listed out the various drugs. The children were required to state if they had tried out any of the mentioned drugs at any time in their life or whether they were using any of them presently.

The questionnaire covered all the drugs that were possible to be used including alcohol, opium, smack, morphine, etc. which were grouped under broad headings as given below:

- Depressants: Analgesics (Ultragine, Metacine, Analgine etc.)Alcohol, Barbiturates (Luminol, Mandrax etc.)
- Cannabis drugs (Bhang, Ganja, and Charas)
- Opiate Narcotic Drugs (Opium, Morphine, Heroin and Smack)
- Tranquilizers (Axum, Librium, Eskazine)
- Stimulants (Amphetamines, Benzedrin etc.)
- Hallucinogens (LSD, Mescaline etc.)

- Any other drug.

Since working children included in this study, in many cases, were illiterate, or just literate, or had studied up to class V only they were all interviewed personally by the investigators and the questionnaires were filled up by the investigators themselves.

Both the checklist and interview schedule were structured. However, taking into account the kind of children in the sample, their behaviours during the interview were also noted down, along with the case history of some of the drug addicted children.

Procedure for Data Collection

The procedure followed was almost similar to that of participant observation as the investigators had to mingle with the children, spend time with them, talk to them at their own level, and even at times take a cigarette or a sip of alcohol etc. with them. This helped establish rapport with the children and made them feel at ease and facilitated a frank response from them. Thus the atmosphere was rendered informal and non-threatening by the investigators who were themselves young in age and who could talk to the working children almost like their peers.

It may be mentioned here that these investigators had been trained earlier on how to extract the needed information from the children. They were all from psychology background and were thus able to handle the interviews very efficiently and effectively with the result that the children came out with the facts and reality easily.

Pilot Study

Before embarking on detailed data collection, the checklist and questionnaire were tried out on a small section of population of working children. In this case they were the boys employed in the university canteen (N=2), cycle repair mechanics (N=2), boot polishing children (N=2), domestic servants (N=3) and street beggar (N=1). These children were not drug addicts and hence not included in the final study. Since they belonged to the age group 5–14 years, and were employed in different occupations, the questionnaires and checklists were tried out on them to establish their suitability. Not many changes were needed. One or two items, namely occasions when they would take drug etc. were omitted and also some of the ambiguously worded items were removed from the questionnaire.

Statistical Analysis

Since the study was an exploratory one, mainly descriptive analysis has been done of the various responses. Frequency analysis and percentages have been used in the analysis. In addition, chi-square test has been used where ever appropriate.

The next chapter presents the socio-demographic characterstics of the drug addicted working children.

III

Working Children, Drug Abuse & their Socio Demographic Profile

As mentioned earlier, there were in all 223 children, working in different occupations, who participated in this study. This chapter presents the socio-demographic characterstics of these working childern. Pie diagrams 1-8 present these factors in a pictorial form.

Figure 1 gives an idea about the native place of these 223 working children. Uttar Pradesh was the native place for the largest number of these children, followed by Delhi and Bihar. That is, more than 80% were from the northern states of India with a very small or negligible percentage from the Eastern part of India. There was no child in this sample from either Western or Southern part of India. Obviously working children in Delhi are mostly from those parts of India which are very close to Delhi. Within the northern parts, UP and Bihar were the native places in about 56% of the cases, Delhi 26% and the remaining 18% equally distributed among Rajasthan, Punjab, Haryana, Madhya Pradesh, Assam and Nepal.

When questioned, almost all children from all these different states replied in unison that they had come to work to Delhi as they could get more and earn more here than in their own states, where they earned just one-fourth of what they were getting in Delhi.

Place of Work in Delhi (Fig. 2)

The maximum percentage of children comprising this study were from North Delhi (46.63%), followed by South

Delhi, East Delhi and Central Delhi in that order. This supports the findings of Veeraraghavan (1992) wherein a similar picture of drug abusers and addicts as well as pushers and peddlars was obtained.

North Delhi area included places like Alipur, Badli, Delhi University area, Keshavpuram, Mukherjea Nagar, Rohini, Shakti Nagar, Tiz Hazari, etc. East Delhi included areas like Shahdara, Laxmi Nagar, Mayur Vihar, Vivek Vihar, Dilshad Garden, etc. This also substantiated the findings of the above mentioned study done in 1992.

Staying With Whom

While many of these working children had come a long way from home, an attempt was made to find out as to with whom they stayed in Delhi. Figure 3 presents the details.

It is seen that 39% stayed with their parents and 34.5% stayed alone all by themselves. Of the children who stayed alone (N=77) it is interesting to note that 34 were from Delhi itself, 25 were from Bihar, 10 from Uttar Pradesh, 4 from Haryana and Punjab and 2 each from Rajasthan and Madhya Pradesh. The 5 children from Nepal and Assam stayed all by themselves. In 17% of cases, the children had only either father or mother and in 9% cases the working children were staying with their relatives.

As for the age group of children the largest number belonged to 9-13 years age group. (see Fig. 8). The mean age of the children was worked out to be 12.78 years with a standard deviation of 1.48.

Type of Family

The type of family to which these working children belonged was ascertained and Fig. 4 presents the details. Even though a large percentage of working children belonged to Northern states such as UP, Bihar, etc. very few

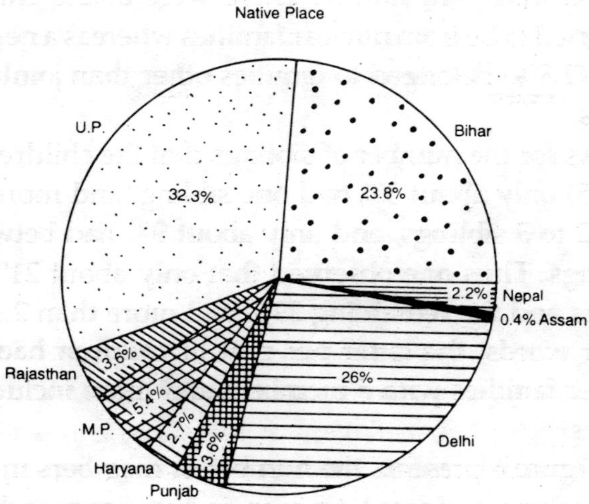

Fig. 1 % Working Children

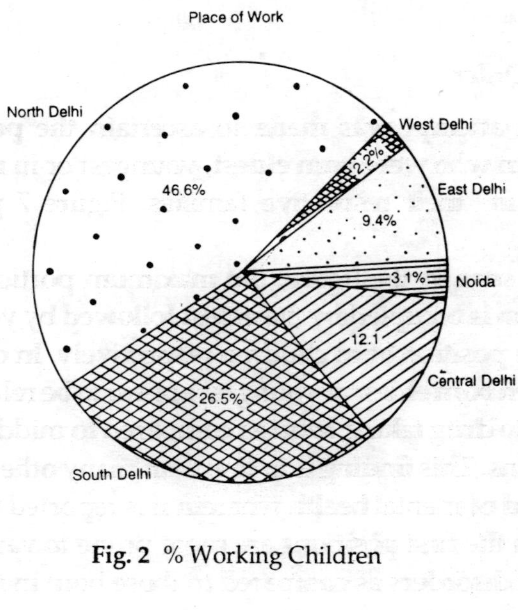

Fig. 2 % Working Children

stayed in a joint family. There were 63.2% children who reported to be from nuclear families whereas a negligible per cent (1.8%) belonged to families other than joint or nuclear types.

As for the number of siblings that the children had, (see Fig. 5) only about 5% had one sibling, and more than 50% had 2 to 3 siblings, and only about 9% had between 6 to 7 siblings. Thus one observed that only about 21% had 2 siblings and the remaining 79% had more than 2 siblings. In other words, the latter per cent of children had relatively bigger families with 5 members and more including themselves.

Figure 6 presents the number of members in the family of working children. As seen in the figure, which is self explanatory, 41% children reported that they had 4 to 5 members in their families. A negligible per cent of children had more than 9 members in the family. There were no children who reported having more than 9 members in the family.

Birth Order

An attempt was made to ascertain the percentage of children who were born eldest, youngest or in middle positions in their respective families. Figure 7 presents the details.

As seen in the figure, the maximum portion of the pie diagram is occupied by the eldest followed by youngest and middle position born children respectively. In other words, children born eldest or youngest appear to be relatively more prone to drug taking habit as compared to middle and other positions. This finding is in line with many other findings in the field of mental health wherein it is reported that persons born in the first positions are more prone to varied types of mental disorders as compared to those born in middle posi-

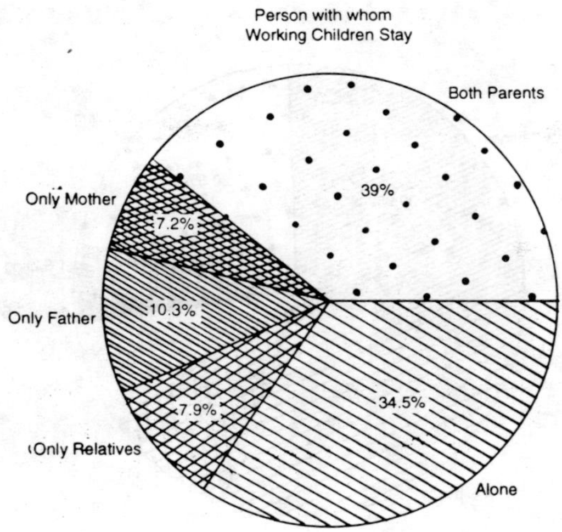

Fig. 3 % Working Children

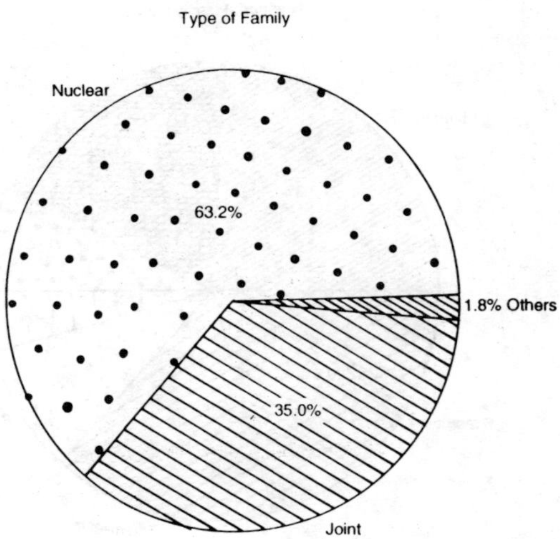

Fig. 4 % Working Children

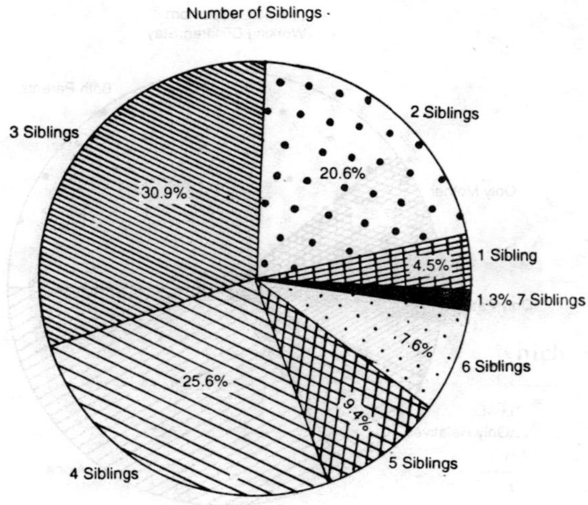

Fig. 5 % Working Children

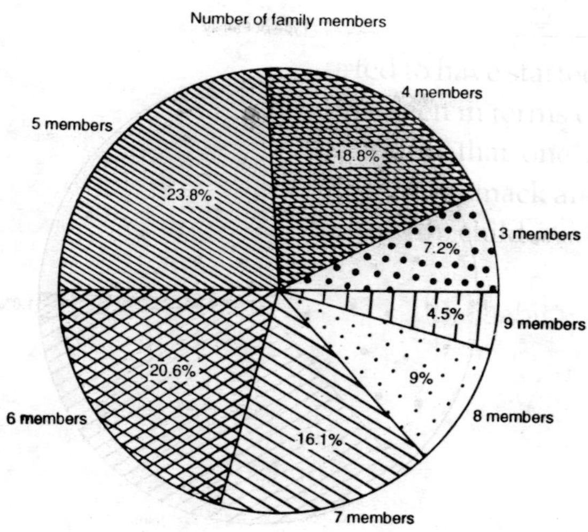

Fig. 6 % Working Children

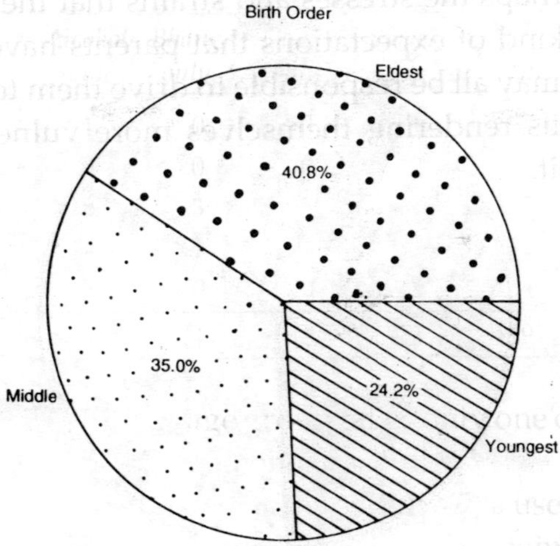

Fig. 7 % Working Children

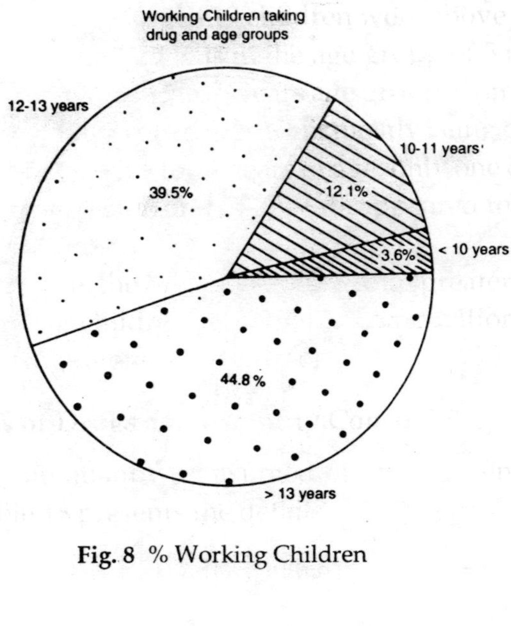

Fig. 8 % Working Children

tions. Perhaps the stresses and strains that they experience and the kind of expectations that parents have from these children may all be responsible to drive them to the cities to work, thus rendering themselves more vulnerable to the drug habit.

IV

Drug Abuse Among Working Children -- Certain Characteristic Features

A total of 223 children were personally contacted and interviewed by visiting them on holidays (Sundays), in the early morning hours (7 A.M.–9 P.M.), that is, before they left for their work, sometimes in the factory premises during breaks, and again in the evenings after 7 P.M. Generally the interviews were held when the employer, parents or any other elder, in whose presence the child hesitated to speak out, were not present.

The data collection procedure was almost similar to that of participant observation as most of the time the research investigators sat around with the children to make the atmosphere very informal and non-threatening so as to encourage them to come out with their most secretive and highly personal information.

The extent of drug abuse can be considered only in terms of the children who have been interviewed. As mentioned in the methodology chapter, the children interviewed were working in tea shops, railway station, carpet manufacturing industry, paper recycling industry, export and handicraft industries. In addition many children were working as *kabadiwala* (old paper/bottle/waste sellers), vendors who sold vegetables and fruits and various sundry items. Some children polished utensils, etc. in addition to working as motor mechanics, cleaners in trucks and buses. Table 1 presents the occupation details of the working children who

Table 1 Occupation of father, mother & self
(No. of respondents)

Occupations	*Father*	*Mother*	*Self*
Vendor*	17	0	16
Kabadi	2	1	16
Agricultural worker	36	1	1
Bus conductor	2	0	12
Cleaner**	0	0	22
Factory worker†	20	0	35
Motor mechanics	6	0	3
Taxi/Autodriver	12	0	0
Servant/Bearer in hotels or restaurants	1	26	1
Skilled labourer‡	12	13	51
Technician etc.	16	21	23
Rickshaw puller	5	0	13
Unskilled worker£	36	6	14
Salesman	2	0	16
Unemployed	6	124	0
Not applicable	50	31	0
Total	223	223	223

* Fruits & Vegetable sellers, milkmen etc.
** Cleaner in buses, taxis, trucks and motor garages.
† Factory worker in weaving industry, paper recycling industry, handicraft industry, and export industry.
‡ Skilled workers includes electricians, tailors, painters, dyers, etc.
£ Unskilled workers includes gardeners, construction helpers, shoe polishers, chaprasis, etc.

were interviewd, as well as of their parents so as to get a comparative picture of their occupations.

From the above table it is seen that nearly one-fourth of children from this sample (22.86%) were working in tea shops, restaurants at the railway station or bus stands, or way-side shops. There were about 16% (N=35) who were working in factories such as carpet industry, paper recycling factory and export industry. If to this, one adds the number of children working as motor mechanics/cleaners/conductors etc., the percentage comes to 33%, that is one-third of the children were working on strenous jobs. In more tedious jobs such as those of rickshawpullers, servants and agricultural workers there were only 15 children (7%), whereas in less tedious jobs such as that of the vendors, sellers etc., there were slightly more than 20% children. As compared to this, the occupations of fathers appear to be more in the agricultural area, as taxi drivers and as unskilled workers. There were 50 children who had no father and 44 children who had no mother. Of the remaining, 124 children reported that their mothers were only involved in housework and were not employed anywhere. While 26 mothers were working as servants in some houses, 23 were reported to be working in some factories. Various occupations enumerated here have been classified into very heavy, heavy, moderately heavy and light in terms of childern's perceptions regarding the nature of their jobs. Table 2 presents different classification of occupations.

Table 2 Occupations classified in terms of the degree of heaviness

Occupations	*Degree of heaviness*
Factory worker, Rickshawpuller, Skilled worker, Motor mechanic,	Very heavy
Bus conductor, cleaner in buses, trucks, garages etc. Unskilled worker,	Heavy
Bearer in a hotel/restaurant; Servant, Agricultural worker	Moderately heavy
Kabadi, Vendor & Salesman	Light.

When the occupations classified in terms of heaviness and the jobs done by the children and their parents are seen the following picture (Table 3) emerges:

Table 3 Occupations of the respondents and the degree of heaviness

Degree of heaviness	*Self*	*Father*	*Mother*
Very heavy	74 (33.18%)	47 (28.14%)	21 (30.88%)
Heavy	48 (21.52%)	50 (29.94%)	6 (8.82%)
Moderately heavy	53 (23.76%)	49 (29.34%)	40 (58.82%)
Light	48 (17.93%)	21 (12.57%)	1 (1.47%)
Total	223	167*	68**

* 6 fathers unemployed; 50 dead.
** 111 housewives; 44 dead.

Only 18% children did light work such as that of a *kabadiwala,* vendor, salesman, etc. As compared to this, about 13% of fathers and 1% of mothers' occupations were of light category.

Thus among 223 children who were all drug users it was seen that except for a small percentage, the remaining children were in heavy type of occupations. These children complained that the heavy jobs exhausted them to such an extent that they started taking drugs to get relief from pain and exhaustion.

Even the children who were working as *kabadis,* vendors, salesmen reported that, their jobs required them to be constantly on the move from morning till evening and sometimes they suffered from hoarseness due to constant shouting. They also reported severe exhaustion leading to taking drugs.

When the child workforce (only male children between 5-14 years of age) in Delhi as a whole is considered, which is 41274 male children (according to the Ministry of HRD, Department of Women and Children) the 223 children, which were clear-cut drug using cases, constitute only 0.54% of the total. However this figure seems to be somewhat on the lower side, as in this study, out of 348 identified drug using children, 55 had to be rejected because of inadequate information and lack of cooperation on their part. In addition, there were children who could not cope up with the work because of their drug habit and left the job. In another 70 cases, the children were using drugs but could not be interviewed as they had to travel back to their homes which were in some far off rural areas and were accompanied by their employers (contractors) who refused to allow the children to be interviewed. Hence a wild estimate of drug using children will be more than twice the number interviewed for this study, which may be around approximately 600 cases out of a population of 41274 male children of 5-14 years who are in the work force (NIPCCD, 1994) amounting to nearly 1.4% children taking drugs.

Types of Drugs used by Children and the Source of Obtaining Drugs

This perhaps was one of the most difficult aspects of the present research as the investigators had to visit the same child three to four times and demonstrate friendliness and confidentiality in order to make them mention the drugs that they were using and the source from which they were getting the drugs. Table 4 presents the details:

Table 4 Drugs taken by the working children

Name of the drug	*No. taking*
Analgesics (Metacin)	1
Depressants—Alcohol	183
....do......—Mandrax	5
....do......—both	10
Total	**199**
Cannabis—Bhang	22
....do...—*Ganja*	54
....do...—*Charas*	11
Total	**87**
Narcotics—Opium	4
....do...—Morphine	1
....do...—Smack	54
Total	**59**
Tranquilizers	2
Stimulants & Hallucinogens	3
Total	**5**
Any other—poison of lizard	6
Trishul (Combination of drugs)	3
Nitrolite (10 number pill)	10
Total	**19**

As seen from Table 4, alcohol was used by maximum number of children, followed by smack and ganja. However, if one considers the group of drugs used by the children, depressants appear to be used by maximum number of children, followed by cannabis and opiates group of drugs. In the depressants category, alcohol was used by 82.06%, in the cannabis group of drugs, ganja was used by 62.06% and in the narcotic group of drugs, smack was used by 91.52% children.

While all the above mentioned drugs are addictive in nature, smack which belongs to the heroin category is the most addictive and harmful drug of all. Children who get hooked on to smack, cannot get easily de-addicted. More than 20% of 223 children used smack and if to this opium and morphine are added, one finds that more than one-fourth of working children taken up for this research appeared to be taking these drugs.

An attempt was also made to find out the combination of drugs used by working children. The combination was not only the hardcore drugs, but also the drugs prepared by children themselves or the adults with whom they were staying as for example burning lizards, rubbish materials used on the back of the mirror etc.

Table 5 gives the drugs taken in combination by the working children:

Table 5 Distribution of working children according to the types of drugs taken

Name of the drug	*Number*
Only Alcohol	88
Only *Bhang*	4
Only *Ganja*	6
Only Smack	22
Alcohol + *Bhang*	11
Alcohol + *Ganja*	23
Bhang + *Ganja* + Smack	2
Alcohol + Morphine	1

(*Contd.*)

Table 5 Distribution of working children according to the types of drugs taken (*Contd.*)

Alcohol + *Bhang* + *Ganja*	13
Alcohol + *Bhang* + Opium	3
Alcohol + *Bhang* + Opium + Smack + Mandrax	8
Alcohol + *Charas*	8
Alcohol + *Bhang* + *Ganja* + Smack	5
Alcohol + Smack	25
Alcohol + *Bhang* + *Charas*	2
Alcohol + Mandrax	2

When the drugs are classified into certain groups, namely *(i)* Alcohol only; *(ii)* Bhang only; *(iii)* Ganja only; *(iv)* Smack only; *(v)* Alcohol + cannabis; *(vi)* Alcohol + cannabis + other hard core drugs including smack, opium, morphine, mandrax, poison of lizard, glue sniffing, Nitrolite pills or No: 10 pills, etc., the number of children taking this group of drugs appears as given in the Table 6:

Table 6 Groups of drugs taken by working children

Alcohol only	88
Bhang only	4
Ganja only	6
Smack only	22
Alcohol + cannabis	59
Alcohol + cannabis + hard core drugs.	44
Total	223

From the above it is seen that there are nearly 30% of the working children who are hard core drug users and only in 14.34% cases, alcohol is not used as the children are taking either only bhang or only ganja or only smack. In all other cases alcohol is a common drug which is taken alone or when other drugs are taken, in combination with them. It is also striking to note that cannabis is not such a commonly used drug as one expects because of its social acceptance and its relative easy availability. However, when one sees the 'only cannabis' takers, there were only 10 children, though in 59 cases, cannabis was taken along with alcohol.

When one considers the tedius nature of the occupations and the drugs taken by the children the following picture emerges (Table 7):

Table 7 Nature of occupation & drugs used by the working children

Nature of Occupation	*Only Al*	*Only* Bhang*	*Only* Ganja*	*Only Smack*	*Al. + Can.*	*Al. + Can + Op + Mdrx*	*Total*
Very heavy	24	1	3	8	17	21	74
Heavy	22	0	0	10	9	7	48
Moderate	19	2	1	1	20	10	53
Light	23	1	2	3	13	6	48
Total	88	4	6	22	59	44	223

$\chi^2 = 18.81$, df = 8, $p < .05$ *for χ^2 calculation *columns merged.

From the above it is seen that when the jobs such as very heavy and heavy are added up, there are 46 out of 88 children, that is, slightly more than 50%, were taking only alcohol as compared to the 19 and 23 out of 88 children in moderate and light jobs respectively.

"Only smack" is being used more by children engaged on heavy and very heavy jobs, whereas very few children from the other two categories of work appear to consume "only smack".

More than 60% of children who take alcohol in combination with cannabis, opium and mandrax are involved in heavy work, whereas in moderate and light work categories there are only 18 out of 46 children who are taking this combination of drugs. The chi-square analysis clearly shows that there is a significant association between the nature of work heavy or light, and the hard core drugs that the children take.

Furthermore, it is seen that those who are involved in heavy work appear to take, in addition to alcohol, all other drugs like smack, opium etc. On the other hand, those who are doing relatively lighter work appear to take more of alcohol or cannabis and a combination of these two drugs rather than the hard core drugs like smack, opium and mandrax. Only two children appeared to be taking analgesics, stimulants, hallucinogens etc. and another three children reported to be taking "Trishul", a combination of many drugs. Ten children were reported to be taking a drug called "Nitrolite" which in their slang is called "No:10 pill". Six children also reported that they consumed poison of lizards in addition to alcohol.

Income and the Types of Drugs Taken

Table 8 presents the income levels of the 223 working children and their parents.

Table 8 Income of father, mother and self

Income	*Father*	*Mother*	*Self*
No income	56	164	0
Less than Rs.1,500/-	83	50	182
1,500–2,000/-	55	7	40
2,000–2,500/-	18	1	1
2,500–3,000/-	8	0	0
3,000–3,500/-	3	1	0
Total	223	223	223

When the income levels of the children were seen in relation to the drugs used by them, it was found that there was no relationship between the income level of the children or their parents in regard to the drugs used.

However, when asked how much money out of the income they spent on drugs, the working children reported as is given in Table 9.

Table 9 Money spent by working children on drugs out of their earnings

Amount	*Number (%)*
All the money	20 (8.96%)
50% to 75% of the earnings	102 (45.73%)
25% to 50% of the earnings	6 (2.69%)
Less than 25% of the earnings	95 (42.60%)
Total	223

From the above it is seen that nearly 60% children spent more than one-fourth of their income on drugs and nearly 53% children spent more than 50% of their earnings on drugs.

Educational Level and the Type of Drugs Used

Table 10 presents the educational levels of working children and their parents.

Table 10 Educational level of working children and their parents

Educational Level	*Father*	*Mother*	*Self (Working Children)*
Illiterate	127	175	167
Just Literate	21	1	30
Up to class V	9	0	18
Up to class VIII	7	3	8
Up to class X	7	0	0
Up to class XII	1	0	0
Not Applicable	51	44	0
Total	223	223	223

Since the number of children beyond class VIII were not taken in this study the remaining were regrouped into three educational levels, viz., "Illiterate", "Literate up to class V" and "class VI to class X", respectively. Table 11 presents the educational levels of children and the types of drugs that they take.

Table 11 Educational level of working children and types of drugs used

Educational Level	*Alcohol only*	*Bhang only*	*Ganja only*	*Smack only*	*Al. + Can.*	*Al. + core*	*Total drugs*
Illiterate	57	2	3	1	34	3	100
Literate CI. V	10	0	0	14	3	16	43
CI. VI to CI. VIII	21	2	3	7	22	25	80
Total	88	4	6	22	59	44	223

$\chi^2 = 61.27,\ df = 8,\ p < .001$

As is obtained from the above, there appears a significant association between the educational level of the working children and the types of drugs that they use. For instance, smack appears to be taken by slightly more educated children than alcohol plus cannabis combination. However when hard core drugs combined with alcohol are considered, one finds here more children from the higher level education group than illiterates. Thus there is a significant association between children at higher levels of education using relatively more of hard core drugs in combination with alcohol or by itself, as compared to children at the lower level of education.

When the children are considered in terms of age groups and the drugs they take, the picture that emerges is given in Table 12 and Table 13.

Table 12 Distribution of 223 working children according to their age

Age group	*No. of children*
5 yrs	1
9 yrs	7
10 yrs	27
12 yrs	47
13 yrs	41
14 yrs	100
Total	223

Table 13 Distribution of working children according to age group and the drugs they take

Age group	*Alcohol only*	*Bhang only*	*Ganja only*	*Smack only*	*Al. + Can.*	*Al. + core*	*Total drugs*
Less than 10 yrs	3	0	0	3	2	0	8
10 to 11 years	12	1	0	5	5	4	27
12 to 13 years	35	3	5	4	21	20	88
Above 13 years	38	0	1	10	31	20	100
Total	88	4	6	22	59	44	223

From Table 13 it is seen that smack and combination of alcohol with hard core drugs and cannabis are found relatively more among higher age groups than among the younger age working children. This substantiates the earlier statement that the lower educational level and lower age group children appear to be using less of hard core drugs as well as drugs in combination.

Frequency of Intake of Drugs

An attempt also was made to find the frequency of intake of drugs. Table 14 presents the details in terms of the types of drugs:

Table 14 Types of drugs used and the frequency of intake by the working children

Type of drugs	*Frequency of intake*			
	Daily	*Once in 3 days*	*Occasional*	*Total*
Alcohol only	61	7	20	88
Bhang only	3	1	0	4
Ganja only	6	0	0	6
Smack only	22	0	0	22
Al + cannabis	50	7	2	59
Al + can. + hard core drugs	42	2	0	44
Total	184	17	22	223

Those who took smack, took it everyday. Some children reported that sometimes they took smack more than once a day. Alcohol was being taken by 75% of working children once everyday. Except one child, all others who took cannabis took it once everyday. Those who took a combination of drugs, took it everyday. Of children who took only alcohol, one-fourth of them took it only occasionally. Thus there did not appear to be any delineable trend in the frequency with which a drug was taken. Children who took alcohol everyday did not take drugs everyday. On the other hand, the regular smack users needed to take the drug everyday and sometimes more than once a day (as reported by some children).

Since frequency of taking drugs also depends on the duration of taking the drug, an attempt was made to find out the age at which the children started taking the drugs.

Age at which Children started taking Drugs

The mean age at which children started taking drugs was seen to be 10.48 with SD of 1.47 in the 5–13 age group. Eventhough the percentage is small (9%), yet 20 out of 223 children had started taking drugs before the age of 8 years, which is rather alarming. If the 223 children are considered in terms of less than and more than 10 years of age, almost an equal number of children is obtained in both these age groups. Since the age of 10 years is too young an age to get into the drug habit, this needs to be carefully noted for policy and planning purposes (Table 15).

When both the age of starting drugs and the frequency of taking drugs are considered together, the following picture emerges (Table 16).

Table 15 Distribution of working children in terms of age at which they started taking drugs

Age group	*No. of children*
5 – 6 years	4
7 – 8 years	16
9 – 10 years	86
11 – 12 years	104
Above 12 years	13
Total	223

Table 16 Frequency of taking drugs and the age at which started

Age group	*Frequency of intake*			
	Daily	*Once in 3 days*	*Occasional*	*Total*
5 – 6 years	4	0	0	4
7 – 8 years	13	1	2	16
9 – 10 years	70	6	10	86
11 – 12 years	86	8	10	104
Above 13 years	11	2	0	13
Total	184	17	22	223

When the children who reported to have started the drug habit at the age of 5 to 6 years were seen in terms of the type of drugs that they used, it was found that one child was taking only alcohol, one was taking only smack and another only alcohol + bhang and the fourth child was using a combination of many drugs.

Table 17 presents the age at which the habit was started and the different types of drugs that the working children were taking.

The above table is self explanatory. In the 9–10 years of age group, there was almost an equal percentage of children taking only alcohol and all other drugs in combination. When, however, drugs in combination were considered, exactly 50% were taking two or more drugs in combination

Table 17 Age at which the drug habit started and the types of drugs taken

Age group	*Alcohol only*	*Bhang only*	*Ganja only*	*Smack only*	*Al. + Can.*	*Al. + core*	*Total drugs*
5 – 6 yrs	1	0	0	1	1	1	4
7 – 8 yrs	9	0	0	2	4	1	16
9 – 10 yrs	28	3	3	9	19	24	86
11 – 12 yrs	44	1	3	7	31	18	104
Above 13 yrs	6	0	0	3	4	0	13
Total	88	4	6	22	59	44	223

and other 50% in this age group takes only one drug and that too in most cases only alcohol.

In the 11–12 years age group, only 47% used a combination of drugs in which alcohol + cannabis combination was seen in twice the number of children as compared to all drugs combined. Of the remaining, most reported to be consuming only alcohol. When smack consumption alone was considered, there were 22 working children, who reported to be taking this drug, of which 19 children were above 9 years of age and only one child was in the age group of 5 to 6 years, and 2 children were in 7 to 8 years age group. Combinations of alcohol and hard core drugs were mostly being consumed by children between 9 to 12 years of age; only one child each in the age groups 5 – 6 and 7 – 8 years appeared to be taking this combination.

By and large, the higher the age group greater the number of working children who took a combination of many hard core drugs along with alcohol.

The Types of Drugs and Quantity Consumed

As for the quantity consumed of the different types of drugs, Table 18 presents the details :

Table 18 Types of drugs and quantity consumed

Quantity taken	*Alcohol only*	*Bhang only*	*Ganja only*	*Smack only*	*Al. + Can.*	*Al. + core*	*Total drugs*
One sip/half a cigarette	7	0	4	13	6	4	34
More than/sip or/cigarette	47	3	0	9	27	24	110
glass/ More than/cigarette/	15	0	1	0	7	2	25
bottle/ more than 2 cigarettes	1	0	0	0	14	13	28
No limit	18	1	1	0	5	1	26
Total	88	4	6	22	59	44	223

From the above table, the following conclusions may be drawn.

Except in the case of smack, in all other categories of drugs, more than 50% working children had taken more than one sip or smoked more than one cigarette. Only in about 14% of the cases they had tried just one sip or half a cigarette. Only one child of 11 years age said that he takes one bottle of alcohol. Thus very few working children appeared to have tried drugs in small quantities. Most children started taking larger quantities in the beginning stages itself. 11% children reported to have consumed unlimited quantities of the drugs.

Availability of Drugs

Table 19 gives the details regarding the types of drugs and their availability as reported by the working children. It is striking to note that none of the children said that the drugs were difficult to obtain. Their experience was that the drugs were either easily or very easily available.

Table 19 Types of drugs and their availability

Availability of drugs	*Alcohol only*	*Bhang only*	*Ganja only*	*Smack only*	*Al .+ Can.*	*Al. + core*	*Total drugs*
Easy to get	9	1	0	2	11	9	32
Very easy to get	79	3	6	20	48	35	191
Total	88	4	6	22	59	44	223

Almost all the drugs are very easily available to the working children. This is a very important fact to note as this substantiates an earlier finding on drug abuse in Delhi wherein the drug abusers and addicts had reported that the drugs were easily available (Veeraraghavan, 1992). Immediate and concerted efforts need to be initiated to make the drugs difficult to get if it is not possible to control the availability of drugs. If the drugs remain easily available there is a potential danger that many children will end up in a few years as total drug addicts.

Causes for Taking Drugs

It is not only the easy availability that appeared to be a cause for taking drugs, but also numerous other causes as presented in Table 20:

Table 20 The causes of children taking drugs

Causes	*No.*
Heavy load of work, exhaustive work, extreme unpleasantness in work, inability to cope with the work load, heavy demand from the employer	34
Extreme cold or heat	7
I enjoy taking drugs	30
There is none to stop me, I am earning and so I am spending	18
Exhaustive work and there is none to stop me	26
Exhaustive, unpleasant work, friends do not let me remain without drugs	107
Dealing with the drugs & so taking it	1
Total	223

From the above it is seen that except in 49 cases in all others cases the working children have said that they take drugs because of severe exhaustion, heavy load of work etc., which indicates total callousness on the part of employers. Furthermore, these drugs produce ill effects on children as seen in the following paragraphs:

Ill Effects of Drugs on Working Children

To find an answer to this question, the effects that the intake of drugs have on children were investigated. As reported by the 223 children, the effects experienced by them after taking drugs for a period of time ranged from very severe to mild reactions and included chest burns, nausea, vomitting, coughing, spitting, bitterness and violent behaviour, loss of weight, dryness in the mouth, stomach ache, itching, exhaustion, forgetfulness, drowsiness, body ache, vertigo and lack of appetite. These reactions were grouped into the following categories:

Reactions to drugs in terms degree of severity as reported by children

Reactions Experienced	*Perceived Degree of Severity*
• Chest burns, Dryness of the mouth, drowsiness, vertigo, body pain, stomach ache, itching, and violent behaviour.	Very severe reaction
• Nausea, vomitting, spitting and coughing.	Moderately severe reaction
• Loss of weight, and appetite.	Mild reaction
• Forgetfulness.	No reaction

When working children were seen in terms of the degree of severity of reactions, it was found that 41% children reported that they suffered from chest burns, and such other severs reactions; 33% reported moderately severe reactions such as nausea, vomitting etc., 7% reported loss of weight, lack of appetite and so on, about 11% said that they suffered from forgetfulness and the remaining 8% had no adverse reactions. Thus, reactions to drugs varied among children and it was thought worthwhile to find out as to which drugs produced which types of reactions. Table 21 presents the types of reactions experienced by the working children by the different drugs being taken by them.

Table 21 Reactions experienced by the working children and the types of drugs used by them

Reactions experienced	*Alcohol only*	*Bhang only*	*Ganja only*	*Smack only*	*Al.+ Can.*	*Al. + core*	*Total drugs*
Severe	38	1	2	7	20	23	91
Moderately Severe	29	3	3	11	19	9	74
Mild reaction	6	0	0	3	1	6	16
Forgetfulness	7	0	0	0	16	1	24
No reaction	8	0	1	1	3	5	18
Total	88	4	6	22	59	44	223

χ^2=30.28, df=8, p < .01

Note: For chi-square calculation, *bhang* & *ganja* were merged together.

From the above it is seen that among those who were taking smack and combination of alcohol and hard core drugs more than 80% reported severe reactions such as chest burns, vertigo, drowsiness, etc. Of the 24 who reported forgetfulness as a reaction, 16 were taking a combination of alcohol and cannabis. As for the 22 who were taking smack, 50% experienced coughing, vomitting, spitting etc. The children who were taking cannabis alone, reported in most cases no reaction to drugs. Thus the type of drugs taken by the children appeared to have a significant association with the type of reactions that they produce (χ^2= 30.28, df = 8, p <.01).

Immediate Reactions to the Drug

While reactions to the long term use of drugs have been discussed in detail in the preceding section, the present section discusses the immediate feelings, moods and emotions kindled up by the drugs that the children took. Among the 223 working children, it was interesting to note that about 35% of them frankly reported that they felt great enjoyment on taking the drug and an equal percentage reported that they felt very high on taking the drug. Only about 9% reported 'unpleasant' feelings. To this if one adds the category "becomes highly sensitive" the percentage feeling unpleasant comes to 14%. Table 22 presents the feelings/moods/emotions experienced by the childern in terms of the drugs that they used:

Table 22 Moods/feelings/emotions experienced by the children and the types of drugs taken

Feelings/ Moods experienced	*Alcohol only*	*Bhang only*	*Ganja only*	*Smack only*	*Al. + Can.*	*Al. + core*	*Total drugs*
Enjoyment	40	2	3	6	12	15	78
Feeling High	22	0	1	12	23	20	78
Energetic	3	0	1	4	1	4	13
Bitter feelings	10	1	0	0	4	3	18
Can't explain	3	0	0	0	12	1	16
Relaxed feeling	2	1	0	0	3	0	6
Become emotional	3	0	0	0	0	0	3
Highly sensitive	5	0	1	0	4	1	11
Total	88	4	6	22	59	44	223

From the above it is seen that negative emotions and feelings are associated with the intake of alcohol and in a few cases with the intake of cannabis in combination with alcohol. It is striking to note that in the case of smack taking children, there has been no report of negative feelings, moods or emotions.

On the other hand in the preceding section wherein reactions to drugs over a period of time were considered, it was observed that reactions to smack were the most severe. Obviously, some of these hard core drugs when taken initially produce very pleasant feelings but over a period of time the effect are really very unpleasant.

In order to ascertain whether the above contention was correct, an attempt was made to find out as to how the children got rid of the ill effects experienced by them, such as chest burning, nausea, vomitting, vertigo, drowsiness, etc. Table 23 presents the details :

Table 23 Measures taken by the working children to overcome the ill effects of drugs

Measures taken	*No. of children*
Go to sleep	48
Put mustard oil in nose and ears	2
Eat coconut	14
Eat coconut and put mustard oil in ears and nose	5
Take disprine	5
Go to work	3
Take more of the same drug	146
Total	223

It is clear that 65.47% of children took the same drug in order to overcome its ill effects and thus ran the risk of becoming more and more addicted to the drug. About 9% of working children took some local remedy like eating coconut, using mustard oil, etc. to get rid of the ill effects. It is interesting to note that 21.52% preferred to sleep to get rid of the adverse effects of drugs.

Despite experiencing ill effects due to the drug habit, the children continued taking drugs. An attempt has therfore been made to find the reasons for such continuance of the drug habit.

Reasons for Continuance of the Drug Habit

The drug habits varied from "cannot live without it", "got habituated to it", "tried but could not give up", "work efficiency increases", "cannot work without the drug", "tension in the family", "group pressure", "taken only for enjoyment", "do not know that it is harmful", "do not know that it should not be taken", etc. These varied reasons have been grouped to indicate the degree of habituation as given below:

Reasons	*Degree of habituation*
"Got habituated"; "Tried, but could not give up drugs"; "Cannot exist without drugs".	High degree
"Work efficiency increases"; "Cannot work without taking it".	Moderate degree
"Tension in the family"; "Group pressure".	Mild degree
"Taken only for enjoyment".	
"Do not know that it is harmful".	

Using the above classification in terms of the degree of habituation, Table 24 presents the reasons given by the working children for continuing with the drugs.

Table 24 Reasons for continuing with the drug habit

Reasons for Continuing	*Alcohol only*	*Bhang only*	*Ganja only*	*Smack only*	*Al. + Can.*	*Al. + core*	*Total drugs*
High degree of habituation	14	0	1	20	9	13	57
Moderate degree	3	0	0	0	3	3	9
Mild degree	4	2	0	0	2	4	12
Taken for enjoyment	29	1	3	2	24	6	65
Do not know it is harmful	38	1	2	0	21	18	80
Total	88	4	6	22	59	44	223

$\chi^2 = 20.64$, df = 9, $p < .05$

*Note: For chi-square calculation, smack column was omitted as it had too many cells with zero.
Bhang and *Ganja* columns and moderate and mild degrees merged.

From the above analysis it is clear that the degree of habituation is significantly associated with the types of drugs taken by the working children. As expected in the case of smack, except for two children, all the others reported that they were "highly" habituated to it. Similarly among those who were taking alcohol in combination with hard core drugs, more than one-third were moderate to highly habituated to the drugs. Nearly one-third of these children who were taking alcohol, stated that they were taking the same for enjoyment and relaxation, while more than 40% confessed that they did not know that drugs were harmful. Thus while the cannabis group of drug taking children did not seem to be much habituated to the drug, most children taking smack and other hard core drugs appeared to be "moderately" to "highly" habituated. It indeed represented an alarming situation.

Methods of taking Drugs

More than 60% of working children took the drug by mouth (orally), 30% smoked the drug in cigarette and around 8% used a combination of both these methods, i.e. smoking and by mouth.

Only 3 children used sniffing as a method as they also used to take mirror glue as a drug.

When the types of drugs and the methods of taking drugs were related, following picture emerged (Table 25):

Table 25 Types of drugs and methods of taking drugs

Methods of Taking drug	*Alcohol only*	*Bhang only*	*Ganja only*	*Smack only*	*Al. + Can.*	*Al. + core*	*Total drugs*
By mouth	88	3	5	22	15	4	137
Smoking	0	0	0	0	37	18	55
Sniffing	0	0	0	0	0	3	3
More than one method	0	1	1	0	7	19	28
Total	88	4	6	22	59	44	223

Alcohol, of course, is taken orally and in liquid form and so also are bhang and ganja. Smack is taken in powder form, orally. None reported to be using the intravenous method. Where there was a combination of alcohol and cannabis drugs, 63% smoked the drugs in the form of cigarettes. Thus taking drugs orally was commonly used method, followed by 'smoking', except in the case of 'mirror glue' which was taken sniffing.

Introduction to the Drug Habit

To the query who inducted them to the drug habit, 61.43% said that their friends did and another 23% said that they were introduced to drugs through their acquaintances. This finding appeared to be in line with the 1992 study mentioned earlier (Veeraraghavan, 1992). Doctors and pharmacists were involved only in 5 cases. Family members were reported to have introduced children to the drug habit in about 17 cases (7.62%). In 13 cases the children clearly stated that they were introduced to the drug habit by drug pushers and sellers.

An attempt has been made to relate the types of drugs with the persons who had introduced the same to the children. Table 26 provides the details:

Table 26 Types of drugs and the persons who introduced the drugs to the working children

Persons who introduced	*Alcohol only*	*Bhang only*	*Ganja only*	*Smack only*	*Al. + Can.*	*Al. + core*	*Total drugs*
Family members	10	0	0	3	2	2	17
Friends	54	2	4	15	37	25	137
Drug pushers	23	2	2	4	18	15	64
Doctors & pharmacists	1	0	0	0	2	2	5
Total	88	4	6	22	59	44	223

As seen from the above table in cases of alcohol and combination of drugs, family members appeared to have played a role in introducing the drugs to their children. Though the number is small amounting to only about 7%, it is indeed surprising to find parents indulging in this type of activity. In a few cases of course the children said that they picked up the habit by imitating the parents. On the other hand, the major culprits are the drug pushers, who have introduced the drugs to the children. They appear to be responsible for introducing smack and other combinations of drugs.

"Friends" appear to be the largest in number in introducing drugs and their role appears striking in the case of smack (68.18%), alcohol (61.36%) and other combinations of drugs (60.19%). Since "friends" belong to the same or slightly older age group as compared to the working children, perhaps a well formulated educational programme might help in keeping children away from drugs even when their own friends try to persuade them to take to drugs.

Reaction of Family Members to Drug use by their Children

In about 64% cases, the working children in this study said that their parents or family members did not know that they were taking drugs; 31 children had no parents; and of the remaining, 23 childern said that they were beaten, scolded and threatened. Only six children said that they were explained about the harmful effects of the drugs and were told not to take the same. Another 21 children said that since the father was taking drugs, the family members did not mind if the son had drugs too.

To the query if the they would like to get rid of the drug habit, 74% said that they would like to, and 23% clearly said that they would not like to be out of drugs, with 3% being unsure as to what they wanted. However, to a subsequent query that if sometime later they wanted to get rid of the drug problem, did they know where to go or whom to approach, less than one-fourth (N = 53) said that they knew the places while the remaining said they did not know. The identified places to go for help included the following: *(i)* Ganga Ghat (10); *(ii)* Butterflies (21); *(iii)* Ashiana (9); and *(iv)* Hospitals (13). It was disheartening to note that the children had no idea about the Navjyoti clinics in Delhi being run by the police department. (Figures in brackets are the No. of children)

Time Taken to get Habituated to Drugs

As reported by the working children, the time taken for them to get habituated to drugs varied between less than 6 weeks to about 1 year. When this aspect is seen in terms of the drugs that the children take, the following picture emerges as in Table 27:

Table 27 Types of drugs and time taken to get habituated

Time taken to get habituated	*Alcohol only*	*Bhang only*	*Ganja only*	*Smack only*	*Al. + Can.*	*Al. + core*	*Total drugs*
Less than 6 weeks	61	3	4	21	37	29	155
6 weeks to 6 months	13	1	2	0	10	12	38
6 months to 1 year	14	0	0	1	12	3	30
Total	88	4	6	22	59	44	223

As expected, 21 out of 22 smack taking children said that it took less than 6 weeks to get habituated to drugs. In the cases of combination of drugs, the percentage of children who stated that the time taken to get habituated to drugs was less than 6 weeks, was between 62% to 65%, whereas in the case of alcohol 69% children stated that it took less than 6 weeks to get habituated to that drug.

It appeared that irrespective of the drugs working children were taking, in most cases they felt that they got habituated to the drug in about 6 weeks time.

Source of Money to Purchase Drugs

Since the drug habit requires considerable money, an attempt was made to find the sources from which the children got money to spend on drugs. In 74% of cases, the children reported that they spent their own money for obtaining drugs and did not approach any one. Whatever they earned, they mostly spent it on food and drugs ignoring the other needs. Most of them slept in parks or on footpaths or roadside shelters. Very few (N=8) resorted to deviant measures such as stealing, pickpocketing etc.

In about 16% of cases, friends and drug pushers sometimes helped with money to purchase drugs, mostly smack and other hard core drugs taken with alcohol.

Thus one may conclude that most working children spent all their earnings on drugs which showed not only the degree of habituation to drugs but also the total lack of nurturance and care given to these working children.

To conclude, the analysis has brought out clearly the fact that working children are taking drugs in a large number of cases and the estimated extent of drug use or abuse is around 1.4 per 100 working children. These children basically are involved in very heavy and exhausting types of jobs and suffer from body pain, etc., and in most cases they are initiated to drugs by their friends. Gradually they get addicted to these drugs. Most of them take alcohol or a combination of many drugs with alcohol. Fortunately, smack is used by only one-tenth of the working children though many take smack, mandrax, etc. in combination with alcohol. Drugs like glue, ganja, bhang etc. are taken by very few childern, though the combination of cannabis with alcohol is obtained in quite a large number of cases. None was found taking any drug by intravenous methods. Drugs were mostly taken through the oral method only. Most children were already habituated to the drug. Many did not know the ill effects of drug intake. They become addicted to the drug by the time they reach late adolescence and young adulthood.

Most children are between 9-13 years of age (refer to Fig. 8) which is the time for studying, playing and developing their personality. They spend all their earned money on drugs at a grave risk to their health. Many children start taking drugs at an age as young as 6 to 7 years. Thus the scenario of drug use and abuse among the working children is highly alarming as can be seen from the case studies conducted on working children who were taking drugs.

The names of these children and the area of their residence have been changed so as to ensure confidentiality and anonymity of the children.

Case 1

Deepak, 5 years old, nearly 2.5 feet tall, works as a *kabadiwala* along with his father in North Delhi, residing somewhere nearby. He takes alcohol everyday along with his father. After his mother's death, his father started drinking. Two years ago, whenever the father did not cook in the evening he gave alcohol to this child to drink as a substitute for food. Since then both of them have been consuming one bottle of country liquor everyday. The child said that he has become lethargic, does not want to mix with anyone. He also thinks that alcohol is his food. He does not want to leave it till his father asks him to do so.

Case 2

Krishna, 10 year old, works in a tea shop as a helper somewhere in South Delhi. He is very active, people really adore him for his quick and efficient service. He came to Delhi from Bihar with his uncle to work. He tasted alcohol for the first time in a party which was held in that shop's premises. When he took the drink, he was not aware that it was alcohol, and thought it to be a cold drink. He tasted bhang during the Holi festival along with his friends. Since he liked the after effects of alcohol, he started taking alcohol 4-5 times in a month. He is not aware of the ill effects of alcohol but feels that it is not a good thing as people do not think well about such drinking habits. He also expressed a desire to leave the habit but not serious about it as the after effects of the drug and alcohol made him feel good.

Case 3

Eleven year old Mukesh Kumar works in a garment export house, and stays with 3 to 4 friends of his age in one of the resettlement colonies in North Delhi. He started taking alcohol 4 years ago. No one in his locality thinks that it is a bad habit or a deviant behaviour. He feels that alcohol is very easily available everywhere without much effort. On the other hand, it also gives pleasure, relieves body pain etc. However, recently, many of his friends lost their jobs because their output in work had gone down considerably. That is why he is afraid of losing his job too and hence wants to get rid of the habit. However, all his efforts so far to give up the habit have not been successful. He said that in the evening when he is resting or relaxing after hard work at the factory, he automatically reaches for the country liquor which is available in a polypack. In the morning he promises to himself not to take alcohol anymore but in the evening he forgets the promise and carries on with the drinking habit as before. He would like to go for de-addiction, but is afraid that if he gets admitted to a treatment centre, he may lose his job.

Case 4

Twelve year old, Naresh hails from Kanpur and is presently staying in East Delhi and works as a rickshawpuller. He works during nights from 6 p.m. to 6 a. m. He started taking alcohol "butter" 4 years ago. His father is literate and works in some office in Kanpur. Naresh came to Delhi when he was 6 years old with an elderly person without the knowledge of his parents. He does not remember why he left home and came to Delhi as he was too young at that time. When he came to Delhi, he was made to beg everyday along with the elderly man and when the man expired, he left begging and started pulling rickshaw. Whatever amount he earns now, he spends only on himself. He does not want to give up alcohol as this is the only thing that makes him feel relaxed, happy, confident and carefree.

Case 5

Thirteen year old rickshawpuller from Nepal, presently staying in North Delhi has been taking ganja and various other drugs in combination for the last 5 to 6 years. He came to Delhi in search of a job, started working as a servant but soon left the job as there were too many restrictions. Nowadays he is working as a rickshawpuller, taking rickshaw on rent from an elderly person, and works only at nights so that the police does not catch him. He is involved in some cases of stealing, pickpocketing, etc. He takes alcohol occasionally but takes ganja and bhang 4 to 5 times a day. He also takes smack in combination with other drugs. He likes to take charas. He and his friends often go to forests of Hardwar to collect charas, bhang, ganja, etc. He was not aware of ill effects of drugs and did not know about the existence deaddiction centres. He said that some policemen were the real drug users and they should be apprehended and sent to jail.

Case 6

Babloo, 11 year old came from Kharagpur. He has 2 brothers and 1 sister and has studied up to class VI. He left home on being scolded by his mother and came to Delhi where he stayed with an elderly person whom he called as "Elder Brother". In the beginning, he thought that he would work earn and save money and then go back home. Even though he worked as a helper in a tent house, he could not save sufficient money to go back home, the reason being that he had started taking drugs like smack, alcohol etc. He has not gone back home and now cannot even imagine of living without taking drugs.

Case 7

Sonu, 11 year old is working as a bus conductor. He acts big for his age, is smart, very friendly and keeps chewing paan all the time like a grown up. He incidentally was one of the children who helped the investigators trace drug using working children. He is doing the job of a bus conductor for the last 2 years. He started taking alcohol 4 years ago. One day when his father and uncle were taking whisky, he stole one bottle and drank up the whole bottle. Along with alcohol he takes smack, *bhang*, mandrex, etc. in cigarettes. He enjoys taking these drugs and explains that it not only relieves all the body aches, but also makes him feel "high". He spends 75% of his money on drugs and the remaining 25% on food, clothing, etc. He often indulges in "Tanka", which means he takes money from passengers without giving them the tickets or does not give the account to the owner. Sometimes, he steals money from temples and prays to God to give him enough money to spend on drugs. He does not want to get rid of the habit and feels that de-addiction centres are not good enough as they do not give freedom to talk to anyone.

Case 8

Bulbul, 14 years old, works as a bus conductor and virtually lives in the bus. He takes alcohol, *ganja, bhang,* charas and brown sugar. He is the youngest son in a family of 5 children. All his brothers and sisters are well settled and none cares for him. In course of time he lost all links with his family. He is concerned about the ill effects of drugs as he has developed patches on his face and body which cause too much itching and bother him throughout the day and night. He wants to get rid of the drug habit but does not want to go to any de-addiction centre as it would lead to loss of job and income.

From the above few chosen case histories of working children, it is clear that those indulging in drugs do not know how to get rid of the problem. They do not seem to have much faith in de-addiction centres and are afraid of losing their jobs and income on being admitted to such centres.

It is evident from the above that these children are crying for help but there is none to provide them the needed guidance and help.

The next chapter presents some of the intervention strategies that could be adopted for prevention of the drug abuse problem.

V

Intervention and Rehabilitation

The preceding chapters have dealt with the drug abuse problem in working children and have focused on the typical nature and characteristic features of this phenomenon. The case histories presented of the drug abusing children have clearly highlighted the problems faced by these children before they left their homes and the problems continuing to be faced by them in the work place and how drugs help to relieve stress and tensions faced by them.

Having discussed the problems in detail, the focus on this chapter is on the measures that could be taken to overcome the problems.

Do's and Don'ts for the Parents

Most parents bring up their children as per their own experiences. One often uses the same methods in raising children that one's parents used, least realising that some of those child rearing practices have ceased to be effective as the milieu and environment have changed. Above all, the parents of those times had fewer opportunities to learn the skills to overcome the crisis or, may be they were not able to recognise the problem at all. If one is a fairly effective parent, children grow up in the right direction, whereas ineffective parenting may lead, at times, to problems in growing up.

Effective parenting can be learned like any other skill. First of all if parents suspect that their child is taking drugs, they should be alert to certain behaviours such as: *(i)* sudden lack of responsibility; *(ii)* dropping off from school; *(iii)* frequent bouts of listless, drowsy behaviour; *(iv)* sudden change of circle of friends; *(v)* sudden development of hiding behaviours without reason; *(vi)* misuse of alcohol, frequent use of it, a lack of control over the amount of alcohol consumed, irrational and irresponsible behaviour when using alcohol etc.; *(vii)* peculiar odour on breath and clothes; *(viii)* signs of intoxication without the smell of alcohol; *(ix)* an odour of burned rope and incense burning to cover it up; *(x)* sunglasses and long-sleeved shirt worn at odd times and places; *(xi)* blood spots on sleeves; *(xii)* repeated attempts to borrow money and unexplained dissapearance of cash and other valuables.

Since the drug problem appears to become intense and noticeable during adolescence, solution also lies in targeting the adolescents and teenagers, so as to prevent this problem from taking a turn for the worse. Adolescent period, being one of transition from childhood to adulthood, demands responsibility and maturity, calls for an ever increasing ability to endure anxiety, tolerate tension, deal with doubt, cope with conflict and live with frustration. Most children manage to overcome these but some cannot face the reality and engulfed with fears of failure, they find solace in drugs — an imagined shortcut to security.

Openness to Try Something New

(i) Being a good parent is highly complex and complicated and it is all the more difficult to remain good during a crisis. Trying something new means to bring about a change in one's own self first. Most people find it hard to change, at the same time, they tend to rationalise their

behaviour in many ways such as : since he (the parent) had not taken any drugs, his child would also not take drugs and even if he does he would come out of it on his own; since he (the parent) gave up alcohol, his child will also give up the habit easily and so on. Perhaps it may be so, but yet parents should be prepared to directly intervene at the earliest and try new methods of dealing with their youngsters. Change is usually a two step process that is *(i)* to introspect on what one is doing ; and *(ii)* to incorporate the introspections for changing a certain behaviour. Parents tend to be blind and least objective regarding their own behaviour, as for example a parent may drink heavily but yet not be able to stop that behaviour and a child seeing him would model the same behaviour and try alcohol. Hence before trying to modify their children's behaviour, parents should develop an insight and awareness about their own behaviour and try to change it so that there is no ill effect on their child.

(ii) Parents should realise that the drug problem starts around 12-18 years and also in children who are not in the hostel but staying with parents and in a well knit family. Secondly, parents should accept the age appropriate behaviour. In this context age appropriate behaviour means, a behaviour which is considered normal, natural and appropriate for that age of the child and here it refers to adolescence. When the youngster shows 'non confiding' behaviour, that is, he rarely wants to talk to his parents about anything then the parents should allow him the space he needs to be himself—they should avoid pushing him, yet at the same time let him know that they are there when he needs them. At this time even though it may cause concern, parents should try to maintain a balanced relationship between themselves and their youngsters. Parents may also have to deal at times with irrational and inappropriate behaviours

such as over reacting to simple issues, getting overly angry, being highly critical, unusual hostility, mood swings and need for praise and support. The parents should create a pleasant environment so that youngsters can discuss their problems with them with a view to overcoming the same.

Family Communication

Much of the behaviour that takes place within the family is based upon how each person interprets the behaviour of the other. If a difficulty or crisis arises, a situation is created which is not typical for the family. In that case it is a new experience. For instance, in the case of parents if they come to know that their child is into drugs it will be a new but a devastating experience. Under these circumstances the child's actions may not be recieved or understood appropriately. It is imperative that the parents should ensure that if the child tries to communicate about anything, they should listen and appreciate adequately whatever the youngster is trying to convey. The parents must be aware of the personal needs of the youngster which in turn will help in solving the problem. On the other hand, it should be remembered that neglectful and abusive behaviour will only aggravate rather than reduce the problem.

Love, Empathy and Understanding to Enhance Self-esteem

Home is a place of learning, caring and a place of acceptance. Parent's empathetic understanding and praise, help children to grow up in a confident and secure manner. The child who is into drugs often remains in anxiety and tension accompanied by feelings of guilt and remorse, and is not able to receive the love of parents. Hence parents have to make extra efforts, use straight talk and express their positive feelings. The youngster needs to feel that he is more capable of positive action so that he can meet some of his own expectations and those of his parents. Since one positive act builds on another, parents should remember to encourage such positive behaviours in their children.

Time

The quality of time a parent spends with the child is much more important than the quantity of time. Time with the child should be spent in a meaningful interaction from both sides.

Value Clarification Approach

The children who are already in drugs may have difficulty in expressing their feelings due to poorly developed sense of personal values and life goals. Parents should help the child to clarify personal values and develop in him the life ideals and enhance his capacity to express and understand his own emotions.

How to Seek Professional Help

It is important for parents to know where to seek help if their youngsters get into the drug habit. Drug information dissemination and drug prevention education are two important strategies which influence the actual behaviour and attitude of the public towards the drug user and also it motivates the user to go for de-addiction if necessary. The mass media campaign is a very effective tool for this, as majority of the viewers include children and parents.

These programmes must direct attention on the problems arising from the drugs, congruent with the social setting in which such programmes are introduced.

At the professional level the rapid spread of drug abuse among youngsters during the past few decades has in one way or the other affected every economic class and social group. Children appear to become an easy prey to drug abuse due to their extreme vulnerability. Research has indicated that the personality traits of those using drugs differ from those of non drug users. Drug users have been found to be more impulsive, masculine and they tend to deny their anxiety and dependency. Intervention thus can be directed at divesting the drugs from their status and towards strengthening the personality and character of the youngsters through different kinds of skill training. At present, there does not appear to be much professional efforts towards meeting this grave problem in children which may become graver with the use of more and more "licit" and costlier drugs such as alcohol and tobacco, psychoactive and pharmaceutical drugs. Professionals should not only emphasize the types of drug abused and the type of problems generated by drugs but also implement effective intervention techniques so as to handle the problems effectively.

It is well known that every professional differs in the theory and philosophy of causation of drug abuse problems; at the same time there are certain causes which can explain drug abuse, as for example, availability of addictive substances, mental illness, personality traits, social inequality, inadequate law enforcement and the loss of religious beliefs, etc.

Interventions

Some of the important techniques used to solve this problem are given in this section. The techniques used in intervention comprise : maintenence doses of a drug to encourage stability rather than chaotic use; gradual and planned reduction of drugs and/or alcohol use; immediate or speedy reduction of use of drugs; relief from withdrawal symptoms; relapse prevention techniques; specific techniques such as social skill or assertiveness training and cue exposoure methods; concentration on physical health issues; individual counselling and use of existing networks such as inter-personal relationships.

Furthermore, there are many centres and units for deaddiction for those who have become addicts and are unable to get over the problem. These include detoxification units, rehabilitation centers, community centers, community based alcohol or drug prevention services, counselling agencies, self-help groups, etc. The aim of all these programmes is to bring about life-long abstinence of drugs/alcohol in order to have better coping style, to set up future goals without drugs, and to increase a sense of psychological wellbeing.

This range and diversity in intervention show that although there are important techniques shared by the professionals, possibly there can be no one set of key principles, methods, and techniques which can be the 'correct' one for everyone. Each professional manages the problem as per his or her expertise. Professionals are expected not only to be well versed with intervention techniques but also to be well informed about certain basic issues such as *(i)* the amount of drugs/alcohol that is considered as a danger level; *(ii)* the early signs of physical deterioration in a child who is using drugs or alcohol; *(iii)* the timing of withdrawal from drugs; *(iv)* the best method of preventing relapse, and so on. Counselling is another important tool to handle drug/alcohol problem and it is not different from other types or forms of counselling. It is not necessary that every counsellor who works with a drug or alcohol related problem be a specialist counsellor.

Whichever intervention technique is adopted, one of the important prerequisites for rendering an intervention effective, is to choose a setting that is comfortable and relaxing for the youngster. The interview should be started in an informal way leading to the problem gradually. A good semistructured interview characterised by fewer questions and by long periods of respondent talking about the problem would perhaps be more appropriate. Increasingly precise questions may be used to narrow down the areas of explanation.

Use of Psychological Tests

While in most cases, interviewees themselves may provide the needed information, in some cases, however, the youngster may refuse to respond and thus the therapist may have to administer certain tests considered necessary. For example, if the therapist feels that the information obtained from the interview is not sufficient to carry out the intervention, or if he detects any major discrepancy in the information provided, or if he encounters a lot of resistance from the youngster to express his problems, certain psychological tests such as the projective tests, kinetic drawing tests and also paper pencil tests, may be administered to elicit the needed information. It must however be kept in mind that the tests administered should match the therapeutic goals. The ideal way to proceed is to assimilate the information taken by medical personnel, psychologist, social worker and then analyse the problem to obtain a comprehensive picture of the drug abuse problem.

Target for Modification

It is important to identify the target behaviours for change which can be carried out by behavioural assesment procedures. In this procedure, an attempt is made to specify the exact variables that need to be modified — they may be situational antecedents, or components of the problem itself or may even be consequent reinforcers.

Intervention Strategies

A successful treatment programme follows typically three phases, viz. *(i)* a base line, or preprogramme behavioural-assesment phase; *(ii)* a treatment phase and *(iii)* a follow-up phase.

Intervention strategies require accurate recording of the data because *(i)* it provides a description of the problem which helps the therapist to decide the appropriate intervention programme; *(ii)* it helps to identify the best possible strategies and *(iii)* it provides means for determining whether the programme has produced or is producing the desired change in the behaviour of the person who abuses drug.

Baseline Phase

During the baseline phase, assessment of the level of severity of the problem and functioning of the individual prior to the introduction of the programme or treatment, is made. In addition to the information obtained in the interview, the baseline data in this context will emphasize on *(a)* how the child became dependent on drugs or started abusing the drugs; *(b)* the subjective experience of the youngster on ingesting the drugs; *(c)* the altered mood; *(d)* whether the drug helps to reduce the anxiety and worries of the child which make him continue with the drug; *(e)* whether the drug in anyway provides an "escape" route for the child from all sorts of stresses and deprivation experienced by him; *(f)* whether the child takes drugs more because of the fear of withdrawal symptoms which can be very unpleasant at times; *(g)* whether the youngsters taking drugs for a long period of time, begin to believe that drug is necessary for their functioning; and *(h)* whether they have developed a feeling that they get strength to face any type of unpleasant situation in life if they take the drug.

Whatever the rationale for taking the drug may be, such habits which are not approved by the society and which in the long run affect the physical and mental health of the youngster, make them feel guilty and unhappy and also bring down their efficiency and self esteem. Thus such self concept turns out to be negative.

In treating this problem, one of the important methods used is self monitoring, which involves the child himself to carry out observation of his own behaviour and record the same systematically. The child is trained to consciously try and note as to what was passing in his mind before feeling a need for the drug and before starting to take the same.

Treatment Phase

As pointed out by Palmer and McMahon (1997), two major concerns are the growth of the drug use by the younger generation and the growing problem concerning drug related crime and public safety. Both these problems demand a greater use of psychological intervention, not only to prevent the children from taking drugs but also to deal with children who have got into drug abuse habit. Behavioural approaches are the best approaches to assist children and their parents by making use of the affectionate bonds, interpersonal relationship and the support system that exist in the family of the child in order to help them abstain from drugs. As pointed out earlier, the intervention should be directed at the child's needs.

Behavioural System Model : A behavioural system model bases treatment on a detailed assesment of all the variables that might affect the child's drug taking behaviour including the manner in which these variables interact. These variables are classified into categories or systems, on the basis of their sources (e.g. whether located in the client or significant others) and whether they are antecedent (*i.e.* nagging behaviour of parents, problem-solving failure), organismic (withdrawal symptoms due to abstinence) or consequent (reinforcement from parents, labeling self as a component) etc. Those variables that are more susceptible to control and which are more likely to yield the best results are then dealt with by means of appropriate behavioural procedures, which might include skills training, stimulus control, consequence control and cognitive procedures.

Skills Training : Skills training requires the following in order to get rid of the drug habit:

1. The children have to learn to think correctly as:
   (a) Drugs do not make people healthy or normal.
   (b) The unpleasant effects of stopping drugs are only temporary and shortlived and in the long run the person can regain health.
   (c) Drugs don't improve sleep or control anxiety.
   (d) Though pain killers exist, they don't help in getting rid of chronic pain, but on the other hand interfere with ability to cope.
   (e) You can always get rid of the drug habit permanently, but only if you want to.

Stimulus Control

2. The children need to learn to keep a diary for a few days to note down the number of times they take the drug, kinds of drugs that they take and the time when they take. The children should be trained to communicate their compunctions for taking drugs.
3. Writing down everything helps the drug user to overcome the drug taking behaviour.
4. Withdrawing from drugs and replacing them with other coping methods such as exercise, relaxation, sleep control, and pain control techniques.

Consequence Control

5. The youngsters need to be educated about drugs and must be taught techniques of relaxation and stress control.

Cognitive Procedure

The family should be asked to encourage non drug taking behaviour in the youngster by praising, rewarding and reinforcing the same.

General guidelines for effective use of instructions:

1. Instructions should be within the understanding of the child.
2. It should specify the behaviour in which the child is to engage.
3. Steps should be simple.
4. Instructions should be sequenced in such a way that the child gradually learns the more appropriate behaviour, proceeding slowly from very easy-to-learn behaviours to more difficult behaviours.
5. Instructions should be presented in a pleasant and courteous manner.

Physical guidance: This is the application of physical contact to induce the child to go through the motions of the desired behaviour. The child should be exposed to different kinds of problems, and to different kinds of problem solving strategies, so as to be able to deal successfully with problems in different areas including relationships and face up to the peer group pressure to say 'no' to the drugs.

Situational inducement : This term refers to influencing the behaviour by using situations and occasions that already exert control over the behaviour and which can be used in a number of imaginative and effective ways:

a. Rearrange the existing surrounding, for example, according to the need of the child change the reading arrangement, sleeping arrangement, presence of the parents in certain demanding situations, etc.

b. Move the activity to a new situation, wherein the presence of certain people, or certain type of work, help the child overcome the urge to take drugs.

c. Relocate people, in which people who are in the close proximity of interaction and responsible for the drug behavior are substituted cautiously and the child is gradually and deliberately introduced to those who do not indulge in drugs.

d. Contingency management is an approach which involves making positive reinforcement or aviodance of aversive events contingent on abstinence. The contingencies are applied by the people present in the environment of the child.

e. Social learning : This helps the child to bring a change in the total approach to life and learn better coping strategies in order to stop the drug habit.

While professional help to drug using or abusing children could be effectively organised as given above, there are certain measures that are needed for a complete rehabilitation of the drug using children. These are presented in the following section.

Rehabilitation Programme

The term rehabilitation in the context of drug use, includes both treatment and other broader efforts to integrate the drug user into the mainstream of the society. Self-help groups and therapeutic communities are effective as they touch all levels. A programme of social developement should be included, especially improved access to education and employment. Rehabilitation should put children back in the environment from which they came but after having equipped them with new techniques.

Rehabilitation of drug using children is a complex phenomena, as it requires involvement of expert professionals at several levels — genetic, neurological, psychological and social.

The development of appropriate programmes according to the needs of children who are abusing drugs, use of techniques of participant observation, etc. would help to identify the real needs of the children and the feasibility of working out a rehabilitation strategy.

The children who abuse drugs are not different from that of any other deprived group of children as the ill effect in all these cases is the low adaptive and coping capacity. The rehabilitation programme, therefore, should include apart from training in better coping skills, vocational training, access to education and skill training programmes which all when handled in a systematic and organised manner will help children develop Confidence in themselves and prepare them for gainful employment in future.

VI

Overview

Drug abuse scenario has been projected by many governmental and nongovernmental agencies, individuals, experts in the fields, journalists and many others. There has been research, general articles as well as books based on actual interaction and work with drug addicts.

The concern of the Ministry of Welfare in regard to this problem especially in the youth, started more than three decades ago and continues even todate. While drug use, abuse and addiction have been considered in adults and youths, almost negligible work has been carried out by experts and professionals in understanding this problem in very young children, especially working children who tend to get more exposed to drugs because of their coming into contact with persons who are looking for targets to sell and push their drugs. Their age is also such that the children cannot assert and say "No" to drugs or to any deviant activities.

In this book the problem of drug abuse among children, especially working children has been taken up using a research oriented approach. The first chapter on introduction tries to bring to the attention of the reader the drug phenomenon as it exists at different levels and the attempts made to understand and deal with this problem. This chapter sets the stage for exploratory study of drug use and abuse among working children.

Chapter two deals with certain methodological issues and puts forward the scientific method and approach used to understand the problem among the working children. Based on the work done, using the methodology, the third chapter focuses attention on the typical socio-demographic profile of the working children, who are using drugs.

Chapter four further delves into the details of drug use and abuse by the working children, the reasons for their using drugs, the typical amount of drugs used, association of the typical drugs taken with the type of occupation in which the children are engaged and earning, their income, the stress they experience, their knowledge and lack of knowledge about the ill effects of drugs on their physical and mental health, the motivition to get out of the drug habit, and finally their knowledge about the services available in the community to get over the drug problem.

Following this, the next chapter presents the details of the various intervention strategies available in the community, with one section entirely devoted to acquainting the parents regarding their role in prevention of drug use and abuse in children.

To recapitulate, using a checklist and a specially devised questionnaire the working children using or abusing drugs were first identified and then interviewed comprehensively to obtain information on the various issues related to drug use and abuse. An attempt was also made to find out their socio demographic background and the typical characteristic features of drug use and abuse. To reach these children, the investigators took the help of children using drugs in certain localities and through them were able to contact and interview the working children indulging in drug habit.

For the purpose of the study, Delhi was divided broadly into 5 zones, East, West, North, South, and Central Delhi. These working children were contacted personally in all the above areas of Delhi and using a specially devised checklist the drug users and abusers were identified followed by a comprehensive indepth interview with them. The findings obtained were:

- The children interviewed were working in tea shops, railway station, carpet manufacturing industry, paper recycling industry, export and handicraft industries, in addition to many children working as *kabadiwalas* (old paper/bottle/waste sellers), vendors selling vegetables, fruits and various sundry items, utensil polishers, motor mechanics, cleaners in trucks and buses, etc. All these jobs/occupations were classified into *very heavy, heavy, moderately heavy* and *light*.
- Among the 223 children who were all drug users it is seen that except for a small percentage (18%), the remaining were in heavy type of occupations. As indicated by children themselves, the heavy jobs exhausted them so much that they sought relief of their aches, pain and exhaustion by taking drugs.
- Among these, maximum (33%) were found in the *very heavy* category jobs, followed by children working in restaurant or tea shops (23%), and children (16%) working in factories. Only 18% children did light work such as that of *kabadiwala*, vendor, salesman, etc.
- Taking into account the cumulative effect of very heavy jobs, there were 46 out of 88 children, that is, slightly more than 50% of children who were found to be taking only alcohol as compared to only about 19 out of 88 and 23 out of 88 children in moderate and light jobs respectively.
- "Only smack" was being used more by children on heavy and very heavy jobs, whereas very few children from the other two categories of work appeared to take "only smack".
- Above 60% of children who take alcohol in combination with cannabis, opium and mandrax are involved in

heavy work whereas in moderate and light work categories there were only 18 out of 46 children who took a combination of drugs. The chi-square analysis clearly showed that there was a significant association between the nature of work being heavy or light and the hard core drugs that the children consumed.

- Those involved in heavy work appear to take in addition to alcohol, all other drugs like smack, opium etc. On the other hand, those doing relatively lighter work appeared to take more of alcohol, cannabis and a combination of these two drugs than the hard core drugs like smack, opium, mandrax, etc. Only two children appeared to be taking analgesics, stimulants, hallucinogens etc. Three children reported to be taking "Trishul", a combination of many drugs, and among these 10 children were also taking a drug called "Nitrolite" which in their slang is called "No:10 pills". Six children also reported that they consumed poison of lizard in addition to alcohol.
- Alcohol was being used by maximum number of children, followed by smack and ganja in equal number. However, if one considers the group of drugs used by the children, depressants appeared to be used by maximum number of children, followed by cannabis group of drugs and the opiates in that order. While among depressants, alcohol is maximally used (82.06%), among cannabis group of drugs, ganja is used maximally (62.06%) and among narcotic drugs, smack is used by maximum number of children (91.52%).
- There were nearly 30% of working children who were found to be users of hard core drugs and only in 14.34% cases, alcohol was not used as the children were taking either only bhang or only ganja or only smack.

- In all other cases alcohol was a common drug which was taken alone or when other drugs were taken, in combination with them.
- It was noted that cannabis was not such a commonly used drug as one expected. However, when one sees the "only cannabis" takers, there were only 10 children though in another 59 cases, cannabis was being taken along with alcohol.
- The mean age at which children had started taking drugs was found to be 10.48 with SD of 1.47 within a range of 5-13 years.
- When the age group of children and the drugs in combination are considered, about 50% of working children of less than 9 years of age, were taking two or more drugs in combination and another 50% in this age group were taking only one drug and that too in most cases only alcohol.
- In the 11-12 years age group, only 47% used a combination of drugs in which alcohol and cannabis combination was seen in twice the number of children as compared to all drugs combined. Of the remaining children, most of them reported to be consuming only alcohol.
- Smack and combination of alcohol with hard core drugs and cannabis were found relatively more among higher age groups than among the younger children.
- When smack consumption alone is considered, there were 22 working children who reported to be taking this drug of which 19 were above 9 years of age and only one child fell in the age group of 5 to 6 years, and 2 children in the 7 to 8 years age group.
- Combination of alcohol and hard core drugs were mostly being consumed by children between 9 to 12 years of age; only one child each in the age groups 5-6 and 7-8 years respectively appeared to be taking this combination.

- By and large the higher the age group greater the number of working children who took a combination of many hard core drugs along with alcohol.
- Those who took smack, they took it every day and some children reported that sometimes they took it more than once a day.
- Alcohol was used by 75% of working children once everyday. Except one child, all others who took cannabis took it everyday atleast once.
- Of those who took a combination of drugs, most of them used it everyday.
- Those who took only alcohol, there were one-fourth who took it only occasionally.
- There does not appear to be any delineable trend in the frequency with which a drug is taken. One does find slightly less number of children who take drugs everyday in the group which takes only alcohol. On the other hand, the smack users seem to have a need to take the drug everyday and if necessary more than once a day (as reported by some children).
- All the drugs reported in this study according to the working children were "easily" available to them.
- Nearly 60% of these children were spending more than one-fourth of their income on drugs and more than 53% of children were spending more than half of their earnings on drugs.
- There was a significant association between the educational level of the working children and the types of drugs that they used. For instance smack was being taken by children who were more educated than others. Also, in the case of hard core drugs combined with alcohol, one found children who had somewhat higher level of education.

- Degree of habituation was significantly associated with the types of drugs taken by the working children. As expected in the case of smack except two children all the others reported that they were highly habituated to it.
- Similarly among those who were taking alcohol in combination with hard core drugs, more than one-third were moderately to highly habituated to drugs. Approximately 33% of working children, who were taking alcohol stated that they were taking the same for enjoyment and relaxation, while more than 40% said that they did not know that drugs were harmful.
- While the cannabis group of drug taking children was not much habituated to drugs, most children taking smack and other hard core drugs were moderately to highly habituated. As reported by the working children, the time taken to get habituated to the drug varied between less than 6 weeks to about 1 year.
- As expected, 21 out of 22 smack taking children said that it took them less than 6 weeks to get habituated to the drug. In the cases of combination of drugs, 62 to 65% of children stated that the time taken to get habituated to drugs was less than 6 weeks whereas in the case of alcohol 69% children said that it took less than 6 weeks to get habituated to this drug.
- It appeared that whatever drugs the working children took, in most cases they had got habituated to the drug in about 6 week's time.
- More than 60% of working children took the drug by mouth, 30% smoked the drug in cigarettes and 8% used a combination of methods such as smoking and by mouth. Only 3 children used sniffing as a method as they used to take mirror glue too, as a drug.
- Friends and acquaintances together constituted 84% of people who had introduced the working children to the

drug habit. Doctors and pharmacists were involved only in 5 cases. Family members were reported to have introduced the children to the drug in about 17 cases (7.62%). In 13 cases the children clearly stated that they were introduced to the drug by drug pushers and sellers.

- "Friends" appeared to be the largest in introducing the working children to drugs and their role was striking in the case of smack (68.18%), alcohol (61.36%) and combination of drugs (60.19%).
- Regarding the reaction of the family members towards their children taking drugs, in about 64% of the cases the children said that their parents or family members did not know that they were taking drugs, and 31 had no parents; and of the remaining, 23 children said that they were beaten, scolded and threatened. Only 6 children said that they were explained about the harmful effects of the drugs and were told not to take the same. In another 21 cases of working children, they said that since their father was taking drugs, the family members did not mind if the son had the drugs too.
- Regarding undergoing deaddiction treatment, 74% said that they would like to, and 23% clearly said that they would not like to be out of drugs and 3% stated that they were unsure as to what they wanted.
- Less than one-fourth (N = 53) said that they knew the places where one can get treatment for drug problem, while the remaining said that they did not know. The identified places to go for help included the following: *(i)* Ganga Ghat (10); *(ii)* Butterflies (21); *(iii)* Ashiana (9) and *(iv)* Hospitals (13).
- As for the source from which they got money to spend on drugs, 74% of the working children reported that they spent their own money for obtaining drugs and did not approach any one.

- Very few (N=8) resorted to deviant measures such as stealing, pickpocketing, etc. and these children were taking alcohol and a combination of alcohol with hard core drugs.
- In about 16% of cases, friends and drug pushers helped with money to purchase drugs and these were mostly for buying smack and other hard core drugs which they took with alcohol.
- As for their socio demographic background, most of them came from relatively poor families and had migrated to Delhi for earning some money. Most of them were from the northern states and a few from the eastern part of India. Mostly they were from UP and Bihar and very few were from Rajasthan, MP, Nepal, and Assam. The age group ranged from 5 to 13 years and the mean age was 12.78 with SD of 1.48.
- There were 50 children who had no father and 44 children who had no mother. Of the remaining, 124 children reported that their mothers were only involved in housework and were not employed anywhere
- While 26 mothers were working as servants in some houses, 23 were reported to be working in some factories.
- Most of them slept in parks or on footpaths or in shelters provided by contractors who had brought them to Delhi for work.

Of the various limitations of this study, the study had to entirely depend on the versions of the working children as it was not possible to contact parents or the employers in this regard.

It was not possible to contact more children due to non availability of contacts to reach them. Furthermore, the contractors and employers of some children identified as drug users/abusers, refused to allow the children to talk to the investigators.

It was possible to visit only the places mentioned in this research. No doubt, there are many more places where children can be found using drugs and also functioning as pushers and peddlars. Some of the street children have been found to be involved in this kind of work too.

Based on the findings of this research, the following suggestions are put forward to reduce if not eliminate the problem of drug abuse among working children.

Suggestions and Recommendations

- Eventhough considerable measures have been taken by the Govt. of India to prevent children from being employed, one finds without much effort large number of children in employment in various occupations. Mostly they are found employed in heavy jobs which again is rather alarming. Hence the first suggestion is that the Child Labour (Prohibition and Regulation) Act, 1986 be implemented in the real sense and monitoring of the implementation of this act be ensured.
- The ILO made a large number of recommendations in 1990 suggesting that children be replaced adults by in selected industries and public awareness against child labour be enhanced.
- While there is no instant solution to the problem of drug abuse among working children, as long as there is a market for drugs, this trade will go on. The way to tackle this problem is to do away with the demand at the consumer level so that there is no demand and so no supply of drugs.
- Accessibility and availability of drugs should be curbed.
- Severe sanctions against pushers and peddlars in drugs should be enforced in the right spirit.
- A comprehensive and concerted educational programme against drug taking should be taken up not

only at the school level but also at the community level with full participation of the community.

- Helping children to get away from associating with drug addicts by providing them alternate activities for relaxation, rest, recreation and exercises.
- Educating children regarding the need for a nutritious and a balanced diet and helping them to have at least one balanced meal in a day. This would quickly restore them back to health and also reduce the ill effects that drugs have on them.
- Helping children balance their budget and educating them on saving money for a higher standard of living etc. as well as motivating them for a higher level of living and functioning.
- Counselling and providing guidance services more meaningfully, focusing on rehabilitation of the working children who are taking drugs or are being pressurised by their so called friends who are drug pushers and peddlers.
- Conducting Yoga classes, meditation and prayer classes to help them feel relaxed and calm and also make them understand that drug trip is merely a passing thrill which is generally followed by depression and discomfort.
- Providing an all pervasive vigilance and control of drugs in all localities particularly in those areas where research has shown drug problem to be relatively more prevalent.
- Strict vigil against smuggling and effective punishments to smugglers, dealers and peddlars would help reduce drug abuse problem.
- The parents need to be educated to take care of their wards and remain vigilant so that their children do not take to drugs etc. They need to be educated regarding the indicators of addiction in children.

- Voluntary agencies should be sensitized to this problem so that they can focus on areas which would help to prevent drug use and abuse by the working children.
- Extensive publicity campaigns through All India Radio and DoorDarshan would help a great deal in sensitizing general public to this problem so that they can report about the same on detecting it in any child in their locality.
- Those parents who are found guilty of not only sending their children to work but also encouraging them to take drugs should be severely punished.
- Since smoking is the first step towards drug taking, smoking should be totally banned and those who smoke should be ostracised.
- Encouraging children from the lower classes and child labour population to involve themselves in sports, gymnastics etc. by providing them financial assistance and incentives for extra-curricular activities.
- Making a provision for a team of trained psychologists, social workers, occupational and recreational therapists, Yoga therapists, doctors, etc. for catering to the special needs and problems of the drug abusing working children, as well as for monitoring the implementation of the Child Labour Act and the Anti Drugs Act.
- Finally it is essential to know why working children take to drug in order to eradicate the factors that are leading to the drug behaviour, and have a well formulated systematic follow-up programme which can monitor the prevention and rehabilitation measures that are in existence.

To conclude, this book has attempted to draw attention of the public to the problem of drug use and abuse among working children and has been able to show that there is drug use and abuse among working children in Delhi to the extent of 1.4 per 100 children which is a very substantial proportion of the working children population. This scene which is specifically related to Delhi should be investigated in other states and metropolitan cities of India to get a clear picture of drug use and abuse among working children. Many measures can be taken to prevent the drug problem among these children and an attempt has been made to present the same in this book for the benefit of parents, teachers, policy makers and the public.

References

Beauvois, F.; Oetting, E.R. & Edwards, R.W. (1985). Trends in drug use of Indian adolescents living on reservations 1975-83. *American Journal of Drug & Alcohol Abuse*. Vol. 11. (3 & 4). 209-229.

Census of India (1981). In *The proceedings of the expert committee on population projection*. National Labour Institute, Noida.

Child Labour (Prohibition and Regulation) Act (1986). Ministry of Labour, Govt. of India, 1994-95 Annual Report.

Dept. of Women & Child (1994). *Rights of the Child: A Commitment*. Govt. of India, HRD, New Delhi.

ESCAP(1990). *Report of the Expert Group meeting on adolescent crime prevention*. Workshop No: 2 & 3, UN, New York.

Government of India Planning Commission (1994). *8th Five Year Plan*, Government of India, New Delhi.

Ministry of Welfare (1992). *Multicentred study on drug abuse: summary of research studies*. published by National Institute of Social Defence, New Delhi.

Ministry of Health (1977). *Drug abuse in India*. Ministry of Health & Family Welfare, New Delhi.

Mohan, D.; Sethi, H. S. & Tongue, E. (1981). *Current research in drug abuse in India*. Vedic Mudranalaya, Delhi.

NIPCCD (1994). *Statistics on Children in India*. NIPCCD, New Delhi.

Palmer, S. and McMohan, G. (1997). Handbook of Counselling, Routledge 11 New Fetter Lane, London.

UNICEF (1994). *Convention of the Rights of the child*. Published for the Govt. of India.

Veeraraghavan, V. (1992). *Assessment of drug abuse and users and drug prevention services in Delhi*. Report submitted to the Ministry of Welfare.

Index